ANCIENT
TREASURES
OF THE
SOUTHWEST

D1506873

ANCIENT
TREASURES
OF THE
SOUTHWEST

A GUIDE TO ARCHEOLOGICAL SITES AND MUSEUMS
IN ARIZONA, SOUTHERN COLORADO, NEW MEXICO, AND UTAH

Franklin Folsom
Mary Elting Folsom

Illustrations by Rachel Folsom

University of New Mexico Press / *Albuquerque*

Library of Congress Cataloging-in-Publication Data

Folsom, Franklin, 1907–
   [America's ancient treasures. Selections]
   Ancient treasures of the Southwest: a guide to archeological sites and museums in Arizona,
Southern Colorado, New Mexico, and Utah / Franklin Folsom, Mary Elting Folsom; illustrations
by Rachel Folsom. —1st ed.
      p.   cm.
   This volume excerpted from author's America's ancient treasures, 4th rev. and enlarged ed.
   Includes index.
   ISBN 0-8263-1427-9 (pbk.)
   1. Indians of North America—Museums—Southwest, New—Guidebooks.
   2. Indians of North America—Southwest, New—Antiquities—Guidebooks.
   3. Archaeological museums and collections—Southwest, New—Guidebooks.
   4. Southwest, New—Antiquities—Guidebooks.
   I. Elting, Mary, 1909–
   II. Title.
E78.S7F5825 1944
970.01'074—dc20
                              93-47282
                              CIP

© 1994 by Franklin Folsom
All rights reserved.
First edition

This volume is excerpted from *America's Ancient Treasures, Fourth Revised and Enlarged Edition* by
Franklin Folsom and Mary Elting Folsom.

CONTENTS

Introduction 3

Arizona 15

Southwestern Colorado 46

New Mexico 67

Utah 107

State Archeologists 124

Index 125

ANCIENT
TREASURES
OF THE
SOUTHWEST

More than 600 years ago 12 or 15 families lived in this 19-room, five-story apartment house at Montezuma Castle National Monument.

SOUTHWEST

North of Mexico no places offer more abundant archeological remains than do Arizona, New Mexico, southwestern Colorado, and southern Utah. Millions possibly billions, of pottery fragments lie in and on the soil. Surveys have revealed thousands of habitation sites. All these are reminders that creative people have long lived here, and all have a common history. The changes that led people to shift from the life of hunter-gatherers may have been gradual at first. People who had been collecting seeds may have discovered that they could increase their food supply by scattering or planting some of the seeds they collected. Once they had garden plots, it was necessary for them to be near those plots at least at harvest time. Life became more settled.

Then, villages, of which countless potsherds are an evidence, came into existence, following a development that took place six or seven thousand years ago. At that time people in the Tehuacan Valley of present-day Mexico, and possibly elsewhere, began to domesticate a certain wild grass. The discovery that they could plant its seeds in garden plots changed their lives and the whole of Indian life in large sections of the American continents.

As this wild grass was cultivated, it changed greatly and evolved into the grain we call corn, or maize. It developed husks that wrapped more and more tightly around the seed-bearing cob, until at last maize could no longer sow its own seeds. It could not live from year to year unless humans removed the husks and planted the corn kernels. At the same time, people became so accustomed to eating corn, prepared in many ways, that their lives revolved around planting, cultivating, and harvesting the helpless but nourishing cereal. Corn and humankind became mutually dependent. The idea of gardening spread northward. So did a knowledge of how to make long-lasting pots for cooking and storing the new food. With the ability to keep food in reserve, diet changed. Dwellings, too, changed under influences that swept into northern Mexico, then into New Mexico and Arizona. Along with corn there came a whole constellation of customs and ceremonies, such as corn dances and other planting and harvest-time rituals. Some of these are still observed today.

Perhaps as early as 1000 B.C. the Western Archaic people known as the Cochise had begun to add corn to their diet. They also added squash and beans. The beans were most important because they furnished protein which would have been lacking if farmers had tried to depend entirely on corn. People could not live by maize alone. Although life changed greatly with the arrival of this extraordinary plant, the changes were not identical throughout the Southwest. They varied from place to place, as communities learned the new ways of creating food while continuing to be a part of the special kind of ecological system in which they had already found a place for themselves. In one sense, of course, all farmers were alike. They could give up the wandering existence of the hunter or gatherer and build more or less permanent dwellings. The differences in the details of how they built and created and elaborated on life are among the things that make Southwestern archeology fascinating to both the scientist and the lay person.

Broadly speaking, four different lifeways developed: The Mogollon (MOH-goh-YOHN), the Hohokam (ho-ho-KAHM), the Patayan (PAH-tah-YAHN), and the Anasazi (AHN-ah-SAH-zee). Eventually there developed several variations or combinations of these four basic cultures.

The Mogollon Culture

By about 100 B.C. the new agricultural way of life had taken on a distinct identity in the highlands of the Mogollon Mountains, which lie across the present border between Arizona and New Mexico. In certain places the slopes of these mountains were ideal for raising corn. They duplicated to a considerable extent the conditions in the part of Mexico where corn was domesticated. Here in the mountains the Cochise had long based their pattern of existence on plant food. They were accustomed to grinding wild seeds in order to make them easy to chew and digest, and it was no problem for women to begin grinding corn as well. We know that the Cochise began to raise corn at a very early date; archeologists have excavated the tiny cobs and husks and even a few seeds of extremely ancient corn in Bat Cave and Tularosa Cave in New Mexico.

After the Cochise settled down and developed the characteristics now called Mogollon, they began to live in dwellings known as pithouses. To make such a house, they dug a circular pit two or three feet deep and set a strong, upright post in the center. Then over the pit they made a cone-shaped roof of saplings which leaned against the center pole from around the upper edge of the pit. Over the saplings they laid or wove small branches, and on top of the branches they spread a thick layer of mud. On one side of the pithouse a ramp led from ground level down to the floor inside.

A pithouse, part below ground and part above, and covered with a thick, insulating layer of earth, was relatively cool in summer and warm in winter. As time went on, its shape changed from circular to oval to rectangular, and it came to be roofed in various ways, but it remained the standard home until very late in Mogollon history.

The pottery that Mogollon people made was at first red or brown without decoration. Later they invented or borrowed many different designs, and those who lived along the Mimbres River developed a unique style. They painted sophisticated, often humorous representations of animals, insects, fish, birds, and human beings on the white surface of their dishes.

The Hohokam Culture

People who lived along the Salt, the Gila, and the San Pedro rivers in southern Arizona also felt the influence of Mexican ideas and inventions. There is no doubt that a great deal of trade went on between Mesoamericans and these Cochise desert dwellers, and much of it passed through a large community in northern Mexico now known as Casas Grandes.

Excavation at Casas Grandes revealed that by the fourteenth century A.D. there were enormous warehouses for goods that people to the north wanted in exchange for turquoise and other gemstones. Copper bells made by a process that had not reached the Southwest, millions of small shells for beads, and large ones for trumpets were stored in the mud-brick rooms of the trading center. Parrots and scarlet and green macaws, much in demand farther north, were actually raised in breeding pens at Casas Grandes.

Before the days of intensive trade, probably as early as 300 B.C., people in the area near present-day Phoenix were developing a special way of life. Known now as the Hohokam (a Pima word for "those who have gone"), they grew corn and other plants from seeds that had come from Mexico, and they brought water to their crops through irrigation canals—a Mexican invention. Later they and neighbors along the rivers diverted water to fields far out on the semiarid land. Rich harvests resulted from irrigation, and the River Hohokam not only had enough to eat, they also had time to spare. Some of them became adept at crafts, making lovely jewelry and figurines. The early Hohokam pottery was buff colored, with red geometric decorations. Later potters made designs in the forms of birds or animals or people.

Early Hohokam houses were somewhat like Mogollon pithouses, except that the builders did less excavation. Later they made large structures several stories high, possibly for storage or defense. They also built ball courts, where they played a kind of ceremonial game with a solid rubber ball, apparently derived from a similar Mexican game.

Did descendants of the ancient Cochise simply adapt ideas and technology that came with traders from the south? Many—perhaps most—archeologists think so. Others, who have done a great deal of work in the Hohokam areas, believe that the Hohokam culture resulted from the actual immigration of people from Mesoamerica. At any rate traces of Mexican interaction with Southwesterners can be clearly seen in such things as food crops, irrigation, building styles, and evidence of religious beliefs.

In the days of the Hohokam there was apparently somewhat more rainfall than there is today in southern Arizona. With more moisture people had more to eat with less work. So life was a little easier than it is for the present-day Pima and Tohono o'dham (Papago) Indians, who may be the descendants of the ancient Hohokam.

The Patayan Culture

In the valley of the Colorado River, which includes the western part of Arizona, lived a people to whom agriculture came later than it did to the Mogollon and the Hohokam. Here farming began only about A.D. 600. In the lowlands on the banks of the great

Ax, Adze, and Celt

Prehistoric Indians cut and shaped wood with all three of these tools, which they fashioned from stone. Each was attached to a handle in its own special way. The ax was shaped by chipping, or by chipping and grinding and polishing. It was sometimes sharpened on one end, sometimes on both ends, and it had a groove which made it easier to attach a handle. (This is called hafting.) The groove goes all the way around the ax or only partway.

A celt was usually polished, had no groove, and was hafted as the illustration shows.

Although neither an ax nor a celt looks very efficient to anyone who is used to steel tools, both work surprisingly well. Archeologists who have tried stone axes found they could chop down a six-inch tree in less than twenty minutes.

The cutting edge of an ax or a celt is parallel to the handle; the cutting edge of an adze is at right angles to its handle. An adze is not designed for chopping down trees, but it is effective, for example, in hollowing out logs to make dugout canoes.

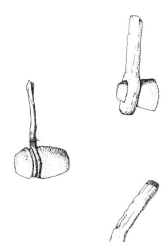

Top to bottom: An adze. A grooved ax. An ungrooved ax, or celt. After Linda Murphy in *Indians of Arkansas,* by Charles R. McGimsey III.

Left to right: Basketry pad, found at Echo House, Mesa Verde, made for use in carrying heavy water jars on the head. Broken arrowhead, found with its hafting intact, showing how a point was attached to a shaft. Original in Colorado History Museum, Denver. Mesa Verde bowl, with a design made in black on a white background.

river, and in the high plateau country through which the Colorado had cut its deep channel, distinct lifeways developed.

Not a great deal is known about these prehistoric people, who are called Patayan, the Yuman word for "old people." The reason is simple: much evidence of life along the riverbanks has been buried under layers of silt brought down by the Colorado River. Other sites have been washed away and now lie, lost forever, in the Gulf of California.

At the time when corn reached them from Mexico, the Patayan lived in flimsy shelters made of poles covered with brush. Later they began to make more permanent structures covered with mud. Finally some of them borrowed an architectural idea from neighbors to the north and began to build stone dwellings.

People who live along the Colorado River today—the Havasupai, the Maricopa, and the Yuma, among others—are probably descendants of the ancient Patayan people.

The Anasazi Culture

Still farther north of Mexico lies rugged country where high plateaus are cut by deep canyons and rimmed with steep cliffs. Here, through the southern part of Colorado and Utah and the northern part of New Mexico and Arizona, still other groups of Western Archaic people made their homes, beginning about 7000 years ago. In one region of northwestern New Mexico, the late Cynthia

Irwin-Williams and her colleagues studied a group whose lifeways
belonged to what is now called the Oshara Tradition. Like other
preferming, preceramic peoples, they hunted and harvested wild
crops, moving about in roughly this one area in an annual round.
Sometime after 2800 B.C. these people learned about the maize
plant and began to grow it in small patches on the floors of canyons.
A more settled way of life was now possible, and with it more
structured social and ceremonial customs, which finally evolved
into the fully sedentary lifeways now called Anasazi.

As the Anasazi culture developed, changes were so very marked
that archeologists have given special names to each of the stages.
The first stage is usually called Basketmaker II or simply Basketmaker. There is no Basketmaker I; the archeologists who named
it have been disappointed. They expected some day to find evidence
of a stage they could call Basketmaker I. They never did. At any
rate these first Anasazi corn farmers tended to live in caves or
recesses in the cliff walls, where their nomadic ancestors had often
camped. Sometimes they may have put up brush shelters in the
caves, and they certainly stored food in slab-lined pits in cave
floors. Later they learned to build pithouses for their own use.
These resembled in many ways the pithouses of the Mogollon, but
in Anasazi country the half-subterranean dwellings had an interesting later history, which is best told at the museum in Mesa
Verde National Park.

These pinnacles, known to Navajos
as Spider Rock, are near White
House ruins in Canyon de Chelly
National Monument. National Park
Service photo by Fred Mang, Jr.

Ancient masonry methods: First, with a sharp-edged blade of chert, a deep groove was scratched on the surface of a slab of sandstone. Next the slab was placed over a pebble. Then, the groove was tapped with a hammerstone, directly above the pebble, to break the slab cleanly in two. *Photo:* Section of a wall built of stone shaped by this method, in Aztec Ruins National Monument. National Park Service photo by George A. Grant.

The Basketmakers did indeed make marvelous baskets. Thanks to the dry climate and their taste for living in caves, a great deal of their fine handiwork was protected from the weather and has survived for nearly 2000 years. For the same reason we also know what these people looked like. They buried their dead in empty storage pits, and in the dry air bodies became desiccated. Men wore their hair long, sometimes in braids; women cut theirs from time to time and used the hair to make bags or rope.

By A.D. 700 the Anasazi had learned more about farming and had drawn together in larger groups than before. They were building houses of stone, one against another in communal dwellings. The Spanish word for these apartment-house villages was pueblo, and so archeologists have given the name Pueblo to the next stages in Anasazi culture.

In the next 600 years the Anasazi grew more and more skilled at building and potterymaking and other crafts, such as the creation of jewelry and fine cloth. Even at this distance, trade brought influences from Mesoamerica. Dams and ditches conserved water for crops. Shell beads and ornaments, macaw and parrot skeletons have turned up in excavations at Anasazi sites.

Within the large, general region where they lived, there began to appear three major centers of development. Each had a style of pottery and masonry and architecture that distinguished it from the others.

One center was near present-day Kayenta, in Arizona. There
the finest achievements of the Kayenta Anasazi are preserved in
the Navajo National Monument. A second center was at Mesa
Verde, in Colorado. The third was in Chaco Canyon, in New
Mexico. From all these developments among the Anasazi one important fact emerges. Using corn, beans, and squash as sources of
energy in an area that was far from ideal for agriculture, people
managed to shape lifeways that became more and more sophisticated with the passage of time. They gathered together in villages
and seemed to be approaching urban life, just as the agriculturists
did in the Tigris-Euphrates Valley at the beginning of the era of
Middle Eastern Civilization. Then change affected the Anasazi
world. Perhaps a series of dry periods made it impossible to store
a food surplus for use in bad times. Whatever the cause, the population scattered.

Archeologists do not agree on what caused the change that left
most Anasazi pueblos deserted forever, but certainly there was a
change.

An Anasazi jar lid. Museum of Anthropology, University of Missouri, photo.

The Sinagua people built these houses in Walnut Canyon, Arizona, and farmed nearby until they abandoned the site for reasons still not understood. National Park Service photo by Hubbard.

A Park Ranger shows how an Indian woman pushed a mano back and forth on a metate to crush hard kernels of corn, making corn meal. National Park Service photo by Robert W. Gage.

Carbon-14 Dating

An archeologist can often learn the age of a site if it contains charred wood or bone. He or she sends samples of the charred material to a laboratory where radiocarbon, or carbon-14, or C-14, dating is done. Carbon is part of the nourishment of every living thing. Plants get it by taking in carbon dioxide from the air; animals and people get it from food, which may be either plants or plant-eating animals. Among the carbon atoms that living things take in, some are radioactive. These radioactive atoms, called carbon-14, or C-14, are not stable. They decay, giving off tiny bursts of energy, which can be detected in a laboratory.

When a plant or animal dies, it ceases to take in food, and therefore it ceases to take in C-14 atoms. But it continues to lose them. The C-14 atoms in a dead object decay at a steady pace. By measuring the number of radioactive bursts produced by C-14 atoms as they decay in a given quantity of dead plant or animal material, a scientist can calculate how long ago the plant or animal died. Since the method does not reveal the exact year of death, allowance is made for error. Therefore a C-14 date is usually written this way: 5,000 ± 250. This means that the date of death falls between 4,750 and 5,250 years ago.

The original C-14 method had its flaws. It could not date back more than 50,000 years, and in order to get a date for an object it was necessary to destroy a large sample of it. As much as ten ounces of a unique bone had to be burned in order to tell how old it was. Archeologists also discovered that they had to regard all C-14 dates with caution, because research had revealed that the C-14 content of the atmosphere varied at different times in the past. Checking against dates obtained from other sources showed that C-14 dates tended to be more recent than they should have been. Archeologists had to develop a mathematical formula for use in correcting all C-14 dates obtained before 1971.

Now another method exists that enables archeologists to measure the C-14 atoms that remain in a sample, not the number of atoms that have left it. This new method, called accelerated mass spectrometry (AMS) finds a date by comparing the amount of unstable C-14 in a sample to the amount of stable C-12 and C-13 that is there. The method has advantages. It extends the range of radiocarbon dating from about 50,000 years to about 100,000. A date can be obtained much more quickly, and the AMS method destroys much less of the object being tested. It is, however, more expensive.

To check the accuracy of a radiocarbon date, archeologists can sometimes compare it to a date of the same object obtained by the use of tree-ring dating (dendrochronology). The date obtained by this checking process is said to be calibrated. Accurate calibration of radiocarbon dates cannot be carried back much more than 6000 years anywhere. In most of North America tree-ring dates do not go back nearly that far.

Advanced technology helps archeologists to get C-14 dates for prehistoric remains. In this laboratory materials containing carbon are first cleansed, then converted by combustion to carbon dioxide in the sytem shown in the foreground. The carbon dioxide is then further purified and stored for analysis in the system shown in the background which operates at very low temperatures. Teledyne Isotopes photo, Westwood, New Jersey.

Carbon-14 dating can reveal the age of things made of plant material, such as this Anasazi hairbrush.

Perpendicular sandstone walls tower above small clusters of masonry buildings in niches or on the canyon floor in Canyon de Chelly, National Park Service photo.

These effigy vessels came from Snaketown, a large Hohokam village site in southern Arizona. National Park Service photo.

Arizona

AMERIND FOUNDATION, INC.

From Tucson (TOO-sahn) drive 64 miles east on Interstate 10 to the Triangle T-Dragoon exit (318). Proceed east 1 mile and turn left at the sign. Mail address: P.O. Box 248, Dragoon, AZ 85609. Phone: 602/586-3666. Open daily except major holidays. Admission charged.

Amerind (a contraction of American Indian) is a private, non-profit archeological research facility and museum. Prehistoric and historic Native American cultures from the Arctic Circle to northern South America are presented in exhibits here. Visitors are welcome to use the nearby scenic picnic grounds.

ARIZONA STATE MUSEUM
(See University of Arizona)

ARIZONA STATE UNIVERSITY MUSEUM OF ANTHROPOLOGY

In the Anthropology Building, on the campus, Tempe, AZ 85282. Phone: 602/965-6213. Open free, Monday–Friday.

Exhibits, which are designed and installed by university students, contain a wide variety of material from the collection of the anthropology department and borrowed from other institutions. A number of displays emphasize archeological techniques for studying artifacts and the material culture of prehistoric people.

Special Interest. Dr. Christy G. Turner II of the anthropology department has examined the special characteristics of thousands of teeth, both in the New World and in the Old, and has concluded that there were three migrations of people from Asia, beginning at least 14,000 years ago and perhaps earlier. First the ancestors of all Paleo-Indians crossed into North America from the area of the Lena river in Siberia; then the ancestors of some Northwest Coast people and of the Navajos and the Apaches moved from a forested area of Siberia across the Bering Landbridge before it was covered by the sea; and finally the ancestors of the Aleut and Inuit (Eskimo) arrived by a route close to the ocean shore.

BESH BA GOWAH
ARCHEOLOGICAL PARK

150 North Pine St., Globe, AZ 85501. Phone: 602/425-0320. This park and visitor center, situated on a ridge 1.5 miles from downtown Globe, is operated by the City of Globe and is completely handicap accessible. Admission charged. Prearranged tours are available.

Salado people, who at one time numbered about 1,400, lived in this 200 room town from A.D. 1225 to 1400. The residents raised corn, beans, squash, and possibly cotton along the banks of Pinal Creek. However, their main occupation seems to have been trading. They obtained copper bells and feathers from Mesoamerica, shells from California and the Gulf of Mexico, and pottery from many places. The Salado people also made pottery for their own use, wove baskets, sandals, and mats from sotol and yucca fibers, and made cotton cloth.

Following a long drought, people gradually abandoned the town and moved to other areas. By 1400 no one remained in Besh Ba Gowah.

Another Salado village has been preserved in Tonto National Monument about 40 miles northwest of Globe.

Special Interest: This large site has been excavated at two different times. Between 1935 and 1940 Irene Vickery directed the excavation as part of the Works Progress Administration program that was designed to provide work for the unemployed. Archeologist Vickery overheard Apaches who worked for her using the term Besh Ba Gowah and she thought they were referring to the ruin, and so she called it Besh Ba Gowah. Actually the Apaches were using words that meant "place of metal" which was their name for Globe—a copper mining center.

The second excavation, which prepared the site for the public, lasted from 1980 to 1988.

CANYON DE CHELLY
NATIONAL MONUMENT
(CANyuhn duh SHAY)

From Gallup, New Mexico, drive north 8 miles on US 666, then 52 miles west on New Mexico-Arizona 264 through Ganado, then 33 miles north on US 191 to monument headquarters and the Visitor Center at Chinle (chin-LEE). Mail address: Box 588, Chinle, AZ 86503. Phone: 602/836-2223. Open free daily, all year. Camping.

Protected by spectacular red sandstone walls, prehistoric Indians built hundreds of small villages and cliff dwellings in this canyon over a period of nearly a thousand years. Visitors can walk to a cliff dwelling called White House Ruin, following a trail that winds down from the canyon rim for about a mile. Other ruins can be seen only when visitors are accompanied by a park ranger or other official guide.

The Story. Beginning about A.D. 350, the canyon was occupied by people now known as the Anasazi, ancestors of the present-day Pueblo Indians. Then about A.D. 1300 the Anasazi moved out, leaving the canyon to occasional visits from their descendants or from the Navajo Indians, who began to take possession of the area. During their thousand-year stay, the Anasazi gardened in small plots on the canyon bottom, where there was flowing water at certain times each year. At other

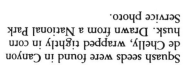

Squash seeds were found in Canyon de Chelly, wrapped tightly in corn husk. Drawn from a National Park Service photo.

Rings, bracelets, bone whistle, pottery sculpture, and carved stone found at Casa Grande. National Park Service photo by George A. Grant.

Opposite:
A Park Ranger examines the demolished walls of an ancient pueblo in Canyon de Chelly. This ruin had stood for perhaps a thousand years before it was destroyed in a rock slide caused by a sonic boom. National Park Service photo.

seasons the stream bed must have seemed completely dry, although there was usually enough moisture beneath the surface for crops of corn and squash.

The Anasazi also hunted—at first with spears, then with bows and arrows. Over the years house structures changed as much as hunting methods. Early inhabitants of the canyon lived in houses built partially underground. Their later dwellings, made of stone and entirely above ground, were joined one to another, so that the whole village was one big apartment house. Still later they built some of their apartment houses in large, dry caves in the cliffs.

About A.D. 1300 the Anasazi abandoned Canyon de Chelly, just as they moved out of other villages in the Four Corners area—the area where Arizona, Utah, Colorado, and New Mexico meet. Why they left is still something of a mystery. Archeologists have discovered that there was a severe drought at about this time, and for many years before they moved away the Anasazi had great difficulty raising crops. Quite possibly this was not their only reason for deserting the canyon. Internal dis-

sension may have caused villages to break up. Or pressure from outsiders may have induced people to migrate elsewhere.

Little groups of Navajos settled in the canyon nearly 300 years ago, and some of the paintings they made on its rock walls can still be seen.

The Museum. Contains exhibits of Southwestern archeological finds in the Four Corners area and also artifacts from later Navajo culture.

The Name. De Chelly (duh SHAY) is a mispronunciation in English of a mispronunciation in Spanish of the Navajo word *tsegi,* which means "a rocky canyon."

Special Interest. Here, in January of 1864, Colonel Christopher "Kit" Carson directed a military expedition that destroyed all food supplies and forced large numbers of Navajos to choose between death by starvation and surrender. The United States Army then drove the Navajos to Fort Sumner, New Mexico, over 300 miles away. There, for four years, about 8000 Navajos were confined in what amounted to a prisoner-of-war camp. In the end, their insistence on returning to their home-

land prevailed, and they came back to Canyon de Chelly and the surrounding area. This traumatic episode in their history is known to the Navajos as the Long Walk.

Fort Sumner, also known as Bosque Redondo, is one of the New Mexico State Monuments, located 2 miles east of the town of Fort Sumner on US 60.

CARLING RESERVOIR SITE

From Arizona 389 in Colorado City drive on a dirt road to Carling Reservoir at the southwest end of town. Mail address: Bureau of Land Management, Vermillion Resource Area, 225 N. Bluff, St. George, UT 84770. Phone: 801/628-4491.

Here several pithouses dating to A.D. 180 have been excavated together with another structure that dates at A.D. 1300. A second site, called the Corncob or Kiva Site, is on Academy Ave. at the north end of Colorado City across from the community center. Here seems to have been a kiva and rooms lined up in a row.

CASA GRANDE RUINS NATIONAL MONUMENT
(KAH-suh-GRAHN-day)

Halfway between Phoenix and Tucson, 1 mile north of Coolidge on Arizona 87. (Note: the National Monument is *not* in the town of Casa Grande.) Mail address: 1100 Ruins Drive, P.O. Box 518, Coolidge, AZ 85228. Phone: 602/723-3172. Open daily, all year. Admission charged. Camping nearby.

This site offers an excellent introduction to the lifeway of the ancient irrigation farmers now known as the Hohokam. A leaflet provides information for a self-guided tour. During winter months a ranger gives guided tours at scheduled intervals throughout the day.

The Story. The impressive, four-story structure that gives the site its name (*Casa Grande* means big house) was probably built about A.D. 1350 and was used until 1450. It may have been a ceremonial center or fortress or both. Its massive walls, made from a special kind of clay, are not typical of the Ho-

hokam. The building is much more like those seen farther south, in Mexico. The usual Hohokam dwellings were separate, single-room houses, made of brush and mud.

Throughout the semiarid Gila River Valley, the Hohokam managed to raise crops by irrigation. They built more than 250 miles of canals, which were between two and four feet wide and about two feet deep. Some can still be seen today.

The Museum. Here may be seen artifacts of the Hohokam people and panels that explain their life.

The Name. The ruins were visited in 1694 by Father Kino, a Spanish explorer-priest, who named the place Casa Grande. The great size of the main building made it a landmark for later visitors, and the name has remained in use.

CASA MALPAIS

318 E. Main St. (Highway 60), Springerville. Mail address: P.O. Box 390, Springerville, AZ 85938. Phone: 602/333-5375. Drive first to the museum.

The museum serves as Visitor Center for the Casa Malpais National Landmark Site which is located about two miles north of Springerville. From there, in summer, visitors will be taken on guided tours three times daily. Admission charged.

Guided tours of the site start at the museum several times a day. Visitors who want to see the entire site are urged to wear boots for a hike to the top of cliffs and to bring a canteen of water.

The Story. Sometime between A.D. 1250 and 1400 Mogollon people built stone houses and religious structures here at the foot of a 150-foot basalt cliff. The land between the village and the Little Colorado River was good for farming, and the site was not abandoned until some time after most of the Mogollon people's little-understood migration to other places.

The rock that these farmers used for buildings was not the easily worked sandstone that villagers found in many other Southwestern places. The basalt in the cliff was of volcanic origin—hard and irregularly shaped when it broke. Nevertheless the builders em-

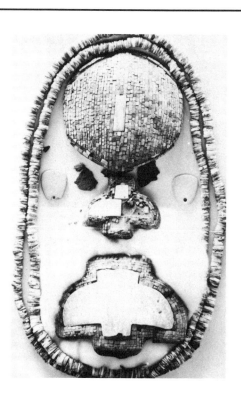

Hohokam craftsmen at Casa Grande glued tiny bits of shaped turquoise onto seashells with mesquite gum. These are in the museum at the site. National Park Service photo by George A. Grant.

This massive structure at Casa Grande Ruins National Monument is made from a kind of clay that contains a cement-like material called caliche. The builders shaped the mud by hand in a layer about two feet thick, let it dry, then added another layer. A protective roof now covers the building to prevent erosion. National Park Service photo by George A. Grant.

bedded small chunks of it in mud and put up dwellings and a unique great kiva which unlike most Anasazi kivas was above ground. Cracks in the volcanic rock, sealed with stones and mud, served as burial tombs. A spiral staircase made from slabs of basalt led from the foot of the cliff to the mesa above.

Vandals have robbed the tombs of the beautiful Mogollon pottery and other burial goods, but excavation has salvaged a few things the thieves missed.

Archeologists plan an ongoing program to interpret the site and explain its relation to other Mogollon communities. As this book went to press it seemed possible that the site might become affiliated with the National Park Service.

The Name. The site has sometimes been called Casa Malapais, meaning "house of basalt," but an elderly resident of Springerville assured archeologists that *Malpais* was the word used by early Spanish settlers. So the name probably means "house of the volcanic badland."

EASTERN ARIZONA COLLEGE
(*See Museum of Anthropology*)

EASTERN ARIZONA COLLEGE EXTENSION
(*See Gila Pueblo*)

EASTERN ARIZONA MUSEUM AND HISTORICAL SOCIETY

Main and Center streets, Pima. Mail address: #2 N. Main St., Pima, AZ 85543. Phone: 602/485-9400. Open free, Monday–Friday.

Salado and Hohokam artifacts from the vicinity of Pima are on display here, together with some material from northern Arizona, which is not identified.

ELDEN PUEBLO

In Flagstaff. Drive northeast on Interstate 40 to Page exit, then north 1.5 miles on US 89 to entrance. Mail address: Coconino National Forest, 2323 E. Greenlaw Lane, Flagstaff, AZ 86004. Phone: 602/556-7410.

At this site, once inhabited by Sinagua people, a summer program for adults and children is conducted by the Coconino National Forest in partnership with the Northern Arizona Natural History Association, the Museum of Northern Arizona and Northern Arizona University. For information about programs and tour, call or write Coconino National Forest (see above).

FORT LOWELL CITY PARK MUSEUM

2900 North Craycroft Rd., near intersection with Fort Lowell Rd., in Old Fort Lowell Country Park. Mail address: 2900 North Craycroft Rd., Tucson, AZ 85712. Phone: 602/885-3832. Open free, daily. Closed certain holidays.

**Twelve outdoor panel exhibits tell the story of the Hardy Site, a prehistoric Hohokam village that now lies beneath the park and the surrounding neighborhood. Partial excavation of the site revealed the remains of pithouses, outdoor roasting pits, work areas where stone tools were made, and pits where calcium carbonate was mined for mixing with mud and water to form plaster for house floors and walls. For other Hohokam sites, see Index.

GATLIN SITE

On Stout Road, off Old US 80, 3 miles north of Gila Bend. Mail address: c/o Gila Bend Museum, P.O. Drawer #1, Gila Bend, AZ 85337. Phone: 602/683-2002.

This National Historic Landmark is a thousand-year-old Hohokam Indian village consisting of a platform mound associated with pithouses, numerous middens, and prehistoric canals. Contact the Town of Gila Bend at 602/683-2255 (Phoenix line, 256-7856) for information about hours.

GILA PUEBLO

In Globe follow signs along Broad Street to turnoff for Eastern Arizona College. Mail address: Globe, AZ 85501. Phone: 602/425-3151. The site is the actual campus of the college. Open free, Monday–Friday.

This large village was occupied by Salado people from A.D. 1225 to 1400. Many of its more than 200 rooms were excavated and some were restored in the 1920s by archeologists Harold and Winifred Gladwin whose home on the site is now headquarters of Eastern Arizona College. Visitors may take a self-guided tour of the site. There is a small exhibit of artifacts in the Gladwin house, but the main collection is at the University of Arizona.

Volunteers at work helping excavate Elden Pueblo at the edge of Flagstaff, Arizona. National Forest Service photo.

In Grand Canyon National Park, Tusayan Ruin, built about A.D. 1185, was occupied for less than 50 years. Then, for some unknown reason, it was abandoned. National Park Service photo by J. M. Eden.

GLEN CANYON NATIONAL RECREATION AREA

Headquarters and Visitor Center in Page, 134 miles north of Flagstaff on US 89. Mail address: Box 1507, Page, AZ 86040. Phone: 602/645-2471. Visitor Center open daily, all year. Closed certain holidays.

After construction of the Glen Canyon dam across the Colorado River, the waters of Lake Powell destroyed hundreds of archeological sites dating from A.D. 500 or earlier to the late 13th century. Extensive surveys, conducted before flooding, led to the discovery of many Anasazi ruins and also of many petroglyph and pictograph sites.

The rock art turned out to be particularly interesting to archeologists. Some of their studies made use of the help of modern Hopi Indians whose ancestors probably drew or pecked or scratched many of the pictures on boulders and on the walls of canyons in the Recreation Area. The meaning of these petrographs (a term that includes both petroglyphs and picto-

graphs) is obscure. The numerous representations of sheep very likely had to do with hunting. Some abstract designs probably represent patterns in woven cloth, since it is generally supposed that men were the rock artists and it was men who did Hopi weaving. In some places, where rather crude work appears low down on rock surfaces, children were possibly copying older people's designs.

Fortunately there are three stabilized ruins on the shoreline of Lake Powell: One is Defiance House in Forgotten Canyon near Bullfrog Marina; another is Three Roof Ruin in the Escalante area; and the third is Widow's Ledge, in Slickrock Canyon, south of the Halls Crossing Marina. These are accessible by boat.

Most of the archeological sites that were covered by Lake Powell have remained intact, and in some cases have become attractive to scuba divers who, of course, are warned not to disturb anything they find.

GRAND CANYON NATIONAL PARK
A World Heritage Site

The park is divided by the canyon into two parts, reached by very different routes. For the South Rim drive 59 miles north from Williams on Arizona 64 to park headquarters. Mail address: Box 129, Grand Canyon, AZ 86023. Tusayan Museum phone: 602/638-2305. For the North Rim drive 30 miles south from Jacob Lake on Arizona 67 to the park entrance, then 12 miles farther to the rim. Open (South Rim) all year; (North Rim) mid-May to mid-Oct. Admission charged. Camping.

Prehistoric people lived in and around this incredible canyon for a very long time. Some climbed into caves in the cliffs and left artifacts there. Dr. Robert Euler has explored the canyon walls and bottom lands by helicopter and has found a great many archeological sites. (About half a million acres in the Grand Canyon have still not had an archeological survey.)

A ruined village called Tusayan (too-say-YAHN) on the South Rim may be visited all year. There are guided tours in summer.

On the North Rim a site called Cape Royal Ruin (G.C. 212) has been excavated and is open to the public.

A third site, Bright Angel Pueblo (G.C. 624) on the canyon bottom near the Colorado River, may be visited all year. The eight-mile Bright Angel Trail leads to the site from the South Rim. Hikers are advised to make the trip in two days. Camping reservations required. Mule trips are also available.

The Story. People of the Western Archaic culture moved into the Grand Canyon area three or four thousand years ago. They lived by gathering wild plant food and by hunting, and they did what other hunters have sometimes done—they made figurines of deer or mountain sheep and left them in caves, apparently in the hope that this practice would bring them luck. A figurine was fashioned of a single long willow twig, split down the middle and bent in an ingenious way into the form of the animal. Sometimes the figurines were pierced by a twig spear, for good measure. Archeologists have found a num-

ber of these split-twig animals in caches in now almost inaccessible caves in the limestone cliffs. Radiocarbon dates indicate that they were left there between 3100 and 4100 years ago. Almost no other artifacts were found with the figurines, so the culture of their makers has remained something of a puzzle.

More than 370 specimens have now been found, not only in the Grand Canyon, but also in Nevada, Utah and California, and at some of these latter sites they were associated with artifacts of various kinds, such as projectile points, sandals, and skin bags. These sites appear to have been used at a later date than were the Grand Canyon caves. The differences in time and the associated material have led to speculation that the non-cave figurines may have served a different purpose. Perhaps they may even have been playthings rather than ritual objects. Certainly people of the Grand Canyon area changed their patterns of living and, in time, became more like the Anasazi farmers who lived to the east and north. Some found their way

Figurine of a deer, made from split twigs about 3000 years ago in the Grand Canyon area. Original in the Arizona State Museum, Tucson.

The Southwest

Only from the point of view of people north of Mexico (Spanish for *norteamericanos*) is the southwestern part of the United States "the Southwest." From the point of view of Mexicans the area lies to the north. Moreover, in prehistoric times the area received attention from people in Mexico and was influenced by Mexican culture.

To prehistoric Mexicans, and also to the later Spanish *conquistadores,* the region was part of a large area that was known as the Gran Chichimeca, which extended northward from the Tropic of Cancer to the vicinity of present-day San Francisco, California, on the northwest, and to Wichita, Kansas, in the northeast. The *chichimeca* was descriptive. It meant, among other things, "nomad." It also meant "son of the dog," or "outlander." Gran Chichimeca was the Great Land of Nomads—people who were barbarians from the point of view of the more sophisticated inhabitants of the Valley of Mexico. Some United States archeologists want to revive the name Gran Chichimeca and apply it to both northern Mexico and the southwestern United States. Other archeologists, having no less respect for ancient Mexican culture and for present-day Mexican sensibilities, believe that the term "Southwest" is so deeply imbedded in usage that it is practically impossible to substitute the older name. So, bowing to current custom in the United States, this book calls the Gran Chichimeca the Southwest.

down the canyon's high walls, built small villages, and raised their crops close to the thundering Colorado River. Others made their homes along the canyon rim. Tusayan, built between A.D. 1185 and 1200, housed about 30 people, but they did not stay long. By 1250 they had moved away, probably to the Kayenta region. One by one the other villages down near the river were also abandoned, and by the time the first Spanish explorers arrived the only Indians living in the canyon were the Havasupai, who have remained there to this day.

There is some evidence that conflict may have accounted for abandonment on the South Rim, and curious settlements on so-called islands in the canyon indicate pressure of some sort. The islands are large areas on top of sections of rock that have been isolated by erosion all around them. These almost inaccessible spots may have been chosen as habitation sites when it became necessary to defend hoards of food at times when bad weather restricted crops. Study of the islands is being continued.

Helicopter rides take visitors close up to canyon walls. At one point below Point Sublime on the North Rim, it is possible to see a former settlement, so protected from weathering that the original roofing on the dwellings appears to be intact.

Visitors to the Tusayan Ruin can take a self-guided tour, aided by a pamphlet that tells about the life and culture of those who built this small village.

The Museums. At Tusayan Ruin the museum has exhibits with special emphasis on the culture of the people who lived there. Displays show how artifacts and pottery vessels were made. There are also exhibits of artifacts made and used by Patayan people called the Cohonina, who lived on the South Rim about A.D. 750 to 1100. The museum is open 8 a.m. to 5 p.m. in summer.

At the Visitor Center the museum is open all year, 8 a.m. to sunset. Displays here show artifacts of most people and periods in the area. Of special interest are the split-twig figurines.

This excavated mound at Snaketown was probably a dance platform. National Park Service photo.

GRASSHOPPER RUIN

The University of Arizona conducts a field school in archeology at Grasshopper Ruin which is ten miles from the Apache town of Cibecue and 52 miles from Show Low. For information about the field school, which gives college credit, address inquiries to: J. Jefferson Reid, Director, Archaeological Field School, Department of Anthropology, University of Arizona, Tucson, AZ 85721. Phone: 602/621-6297 or 8546.

HARDY SITE

(See Fort Lowell City Park Museum)

HEARD MUSEUM OF NATIVE CULTURES AND ART

22 E. Monte Vista Road, Phoenix, AZ 85004. Phone: 602/252-8840. Open Monday–Saturday; afternoon, Sunday. Closed certain holidays. Admission charged.

Collections in this museum are built around the artifacts and life of Native Americans of the Southwest.

HOMOLOVI RUINS STATE PARK

From Winslow drive 5 miles southwest on Arizona 87. Mail address: 523 West 2nd St., Winslow, AZ 86047. Phone: 602/289-4106. Open Monday–Friday, all year. Admission charged. Camping.

As this book went to press this park was scheduled to open. Six archeological sites in the park were occupied between A.D. 1250 and 1600. The area was a stopping place for the Hopis when they were migrating toward the mesas where they now live.

KEET SEEL

(See Navajo National Monument)

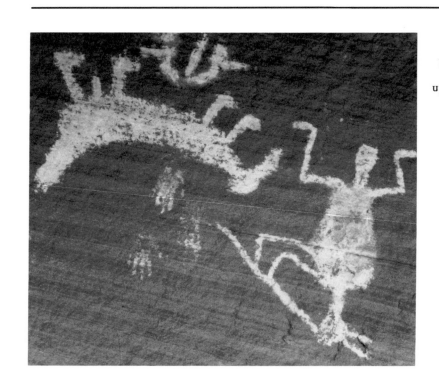

Kokopelli with dog. A petroglyph in Many Cherries Canyon, Canyon del Muerto, Canyon de Chelly National Monument. Photo by Bob Powell; copyright by Bob Powell.

Dogs and Prehistoric Americans

No one knows when dogs first appeared in North America. They had already been domesticated by people who camped at the Koster Site in Illinois, about 5000 B.C. They may have been used by hunters to help in pursuing game, but there is no doubt that they were companions for adults and playmates for children. Among some tribes they had an important place in religious ceremonies. Occasionally they were sacrificed, in somewhat the same way that animals were sacrificed in biblical times, and were ritually buried. Sometimes they were eaten ceremonially—or simply as food in some areas, particularly in the Southwest. On the Northwest Coast people raised a special, long-haired breed and used the hair in weaving blankets and belts.

Dogs were known throughout much of America, especially where men were hunters. In some farming areas archeologists have found no skeletons at all to indicate their presence, but wherever they existed they were the most important domesticated animal—often the only domesticated one. In the Plains area they carried loads on special pole frames called travois (truh-VOY).

One curious fact: In many places the very earliest dogs were very small. Later, dogs in the warmer parts of the continent were small, but farther north they were large, and the largest of all lived farthest north.

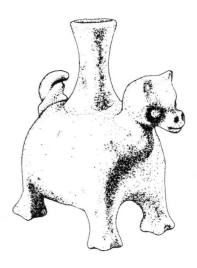

Pottery in the form of a dog made by an artist of the Mississippian culture in Tennessee. Original in the Peabody Museum, Harvard University.

KINISHBA PUEBLO

Mail address: White Mountain Apache Tribal Headquarters, Box 507, Fort Apache, AZ 85926. Phone at Apache Culture Center: 602/338-4625. The site is 3 miles from Fort Apache. Open free, all year.

This partly restored Mogollon-Anasazi pueblo housed a thousand or more people between A.D. 1100 and 1350. It is one of the largest ruins in the Southwest. Despite its importance, the pueblo can only be viewed through a barbed-wire fence, which the White Mountain Apache Tribe has put up for the safety of visitors and for the protection of the site. When funds become available the tribe hopes to stabilize and restore the entire town, which includes two enclosed courtyards, and to reestablish the museum it once operated here.

Special Interest. An early excavator at Kinishba found the skeleton of a child around which was wrapped a necklace almost six feet long, made of 2,534 carefully polished turquoise beads. This astonishing piece of work is now in the Arizona State Museum at Tucson. Also in the necklace were 11 larger beads made of catlinite (pipestone), which may have been brought by traders from far-away Minnesota. Many other necklaces at Kinishba included coral, which came from either the Gulf of Mexico or Baja California, and shells from the Pacific Coast. Trade was obviously extensive in prehistoric America.

KINLICHEE TRIBAL PARK

On the Navajo Indian Reservation, drive west from Window Rock 22 miles on Navajo 3 (Arizona 264) to Cross Canyon Trading Post, then 2.5 miles north on a gravel road to Kinlichee and Cross Canyon Ruins. Mail address: Parks and Recreation Department, P.O. Box 308, Window Rock, AZ 86515. Phone: 602/871-6436. Open free, at all times. Camping nearby. Fee for camping charged.

Anasazi people lived in this area for more than 500 years. Today, in a Tribal Park, the Navajo Indians are preserving the ruins of Anasazi dwellings, the oldest of which is a pithouse dated at

Paleo and Archaic

Paleo-Indian is the term used for the First Americans. They got their subsistence from various sources, but their special achievement seems to have been as hunters of herding animals, which were often very large. The Paleo way of life ended as the herds of big game disappeared. By 6000 B.C. it was necessary to exploit every available food resource to the maximum.

Smaller animals, edible plants, fish, and shellfish now became the fare of people who followed what is called the Archaic lifeway. They hunted and foraged characteristically in forested areas in the East and in semiarid regions in the West, but their lifeways spread over the entire continent.

Out of the Archaic, beginning about 1000 B.C., or perhaps a little earlier, there developed cultures that practiced gardening. People in many places began to create at least part of their food supply, and this meant that they became more and more settled village dwellers. The older lifeways persisted in areas not suited to food growing, but Indian farms and towns were widespread by the time Europeans mistakenly labeled them Indian.

Montezuma Castle ruin was given its name by early white settlers, who mistakenly guessed that Aztec Indians had built the cliff dwellings here. Santa Fe Railway photo.

about A.D. 800. Other ruins belong to the various Pueblo periods up to about 1300, when the large, apartment-house villages were abandoned. Wayside exhibits and a trail take the visitor on a self-guided tour, which gives an opportunity to see how Anasazi architecture evolved. To help visitors visualize the life of the past one of the ruins has been completely reconstructed.

MARANA MOUND

In the vicinity of Phoenix, AZ. Earthwatch is under the direction of Dr. Paul Fish, Suzanne Fish and Dr. Curtiss Brennan of the Arizona State Museum. The University of Arizona conducts excavation at this Hohokam ceremonial mound and the surrounding area. For information about fees and how to participate in this dig apply to: Earthwatch, 680 Mount Auburn St., Box 403, Waterton, MA 02272. Phone: 617/926-8200.

MESA SOUTHWEST MUSEUM

53 North Macdonald, Mesa, AZ 85201. Phone: 602/644-2230. Open Tuesday–Saturday; afternoon, Sunday. Admission charged.

Full-size replicas of Hohokam and Salado dwellings form part of the museum's permanent exhibits which tell the story of the farming people who lived in the Salt River Valley from about A.D. 400 to 1450.

MONTEZUMA CASTLE
NATIONAL MONUMENT

From Flagstaff drive 50 miles south on Interstate 17, then 2.5 miles east to the Visitor Center. Mail address: P.O. Box 219, Camp Verde, AZ 86322. Phone: 602/567-3322. Open daily, all year. Admission charged.

The monument is in two sections—Montezuma Castle and Montezuma Well, 9.5 miles apart. Footpaths from headquarters building lead toward the beautifully preserved "castle," a cliff dwelling built a hundred feet above the valley floor. Along the walk is a

Montezuma Castle. National Park Service photo by Dave Roberts.

diorama with audio tape that explains what life was like in the dwelling more than 600 years ago. The ledge that supports the buildings has weathered so greatly that visits to the castle itself are no longer permitted. Ruins of other dwellings at the foot of the cliff, farther along the trail, may be visited.

At Montezuma Well two ruins overlook a sunken lake, about 400 feet across and 55 feet deep. The well is fed by a huge spring, from which flow 1 1/2 million gallons of water every day.

The Story. Farmers with different customs contributed to the development of a distinct way of life in the valley of the Verde River. About A.D. 600 a group of Hohokam people moved into the valley from the desert country near modern Phoenix, where they lived in one-family, one-room houses made of poles covered with brush and mud. The Hohokam were farmers who dug irrigation canals to water their crops of corn, squash, beans, and cotton.

A second group of farmers lived north of the Verde Valley. These people, who raised crops without irrigation, have been named the Sinagua (sin-AH-wah), Spanish for "without water."

About A.D. 1150 rainfall increased and water-conserving practices improved. Trade in copper and cotton also increased, and the population grew. People began to build stone houses in the cliff overhangs, Anasazi-fashion. Then by about A.D. 1250 the people left these buildings, no one knows why, and moved off to the southeast.

The Name. Early white settlers in the Verde Valley mistakenly thought that Aztec Indians had built the dwellings at this site. So the five-story apartment house and the well, several miles away, were both named in honor of Montezuma, last Aztec emperor. The name, although misleading, has stuck.

Special Feature. The prehistoric farmers here built irrigation canals from Montezuma Well to their garden plots. Because the water contained lime, the ditches became lined with a hard cement-like crust, which has survived to this day.

Could a Clovis Point Kill a Mammoth?

Because mammoths are extinct there is no way to experiment on them. However, some of these prehistoric elephants have been preserved in a frozen state in Siberia, so we know that a mammoth hide was about as thick as a present-day elephant hide and that the two animals were very similar in other ways.

Fortunately for archeologists, officials in a national park in Zimbabwe in southern Africa decided it was necessary to reduce the size of the elephant population. They allowed George C. Frison of the University of Wyoming to help them, using replicated Clovis points. In 1984 and again in 1985 Frison established that Clovis points on darts propelled by atlatls could indeed kill the largest of land mammals.

In 1990 archeologists found blood on an 11,000-year-old Clovis point excavated in the state of Washington. Tests showed that this blood did not come from a mammoth but from a human being. Did a mammoth hunter cut his finger when he was making a Clovis point or is this blood evidence of prehistoric warfare? We are not likely ever to know the answer to that question.

MUSEUM OF ANTHROPOLOGY

Eastern Arizona College, 345 College Ave., Thatcher, AZ 85552. Phone: 602/428-1133, ext. 310. Open free Monday–Friday. Closed in summer.

Exhibits here specialize in the archeology of southeastern Arizona and include a stratigraphic depiction of Gila Valley prehistory, functional replicas of Indian weaponry and a diorama of late Ice Age Arizona. The museum offers visitors a chance to grind corn, drill shells and start a fire with a bow drill. Guided tours are available.

MUSEUM OF NORTHERN ARIZONA

Fort Valley Rd. (US 180), Flagstaff. Mail address: Rte 4, Box 720, Flagstaff, AZ 86001. Phone: 602/774-5211. Open free, Monday–Saturday; afternoon, Sunday. Closed certain holidays.

Excellent displays on prehistoric and contemporary native cultures of the Colorado Plateau cover all periods from the Paleo-Indian, Anasazi and Pueblo, through present-day Hopi and Navajo cultures.

MONUMENT VALLEY NAVAJO TRIBAL PARK

From Kayenta drive 24 miles north on US 191 to directional sign, then 5 miles east on local road to Visitor Center. Mail address: P.O. Box 360289, Monument Valley, UT 84536. Phone: 801/727-3287. Open free, all year.

At the Visitor Center in this Navajo Tribal Park arrangements can be made for guided four-wheel drive trips to prehistoric ruins in the Monument Valley area.

MURRAY SPRINGS CLOVIS SITE

San Pedro Project Office, Bureau of Land Management, Rural Route 1, Box 9853, Huachuca City, AZ 85616. Phone: 602/457-2265.

Paleo-Indians camped here and killed and butchered mammoth and bison. The site was not yet open as this book went to press. Inquire about opening date and road directions at the address above.

Clovis points, named for the site near Clovis, New Mexico, where they were first found, appear in a very wide area. These parts of Clovis points are from a site in Virginia. Thunderbird Research Corporation photo.

NAVAJO COMMUNITY COLLEGE NED HATATHLI CENTER

On the college campus. From US 191 at Round Rock drive 22 miles south on Navajo Route 12 past Lukachukai, then right on Navajo Route 64 and first left on spur leading to the college. Mail address: Tsaile, AZ 86556. Phone: 602/724-3311. Open free, Sunday–Friday; morning Saturday, during the college year.

Displays contain Navajo sand paintings and other materials, together with artifacts from other Indian cultures. This college was the first to be located on a reservation and controlled by Native American people.

NAVAJO NATIONAL MONUMENT

From Tuba City drive 56 miles northeast on US 160, then 9 miles northwest on a paved road to the Visitor Center. Mail address: HC 71, Box 3, Tonalea, AZ 86044-9704. Phone: 602/672-2366. Open free, daily, all year. Camping.

Here several superb cliff dwellings may be visited. Tours are conducted in spring, summer, and fall to the most accessible ruin, Betatakin (be-TAH-tah-kin), which means "ledge house" in the language of the Navajos, who inhabit the region today. This is a village of 135 rooms, built in an immense cave, which reaches 500 feet in height.

Another ruin, one of the largest in Arizona, is Keet Seel, which means "broken pottery" in the Navajo language. An eight-mile trail leads down into a canyon and along a stream to this splendid cliff village, which has a remarkably new appearance, although its 160 rooms have not been lived in for more than 600 years. A visit to Keet Seel takes a full day on horses, which can be rented from Navajos, or two days on foot, with an overnight stay in the campground near the ruin. Only 1500 visitors a year are allowed at Keet Seel. Tours of the ruin are conducted by a park ranger. Make advance arrangement for horses and/or a tour by writing to Monument Headquarters.

The Story. About 1500 years ago a special way of life began to develop in northern Arizona and New Mexico and in southern Colorado. People there had learned to farm, and so they could settle in small, permanent villages, which were scattered over a very large area. Little by little these communities joined to form bigger ones, and finally the population became oriented around three distinct cultural regions. One centered at Mesa Verde in Colorado, another at Chaco Canyon, in New Mexico, and the third near Kayenta, in Arizona. All of these people shared certain characteristics, and they have been given the general name Anasazi.

The Kayenta branch of the Anasazi built Betatakin, Keet Seel, and a dwelling called Inscription House (not open to visitors). Like many Anasazi villages these were abandoned in the late 1200s for reasons that are little understood.

Modern Navajo Indians, for whom the monument is named, avoided the ruins because they feared all things dead. Then in the nineteenth century John Wetherill, a trader with the Indians, and Byron Cummings, an archeologist, visited Betatakin and Inscription House. John Wetherill's brother Richard later discovered Keet Seel.

Special Feature. In the museum at the Visitor Center an audio-visual program shows how the Anasazi lived and what they made. In summer there are campfire programs, which introduce visitors to the history and archeology of the monument.

NAVAJO TRIBAL MUSEUM

Navajo Arts and Crafts Enterprise Bldg., on Arizona 264, Window Rock. Mail address: P.O. Box 308, Window Rock, AZ 86515. Phone: 602/871-6673. Open free, Monday–Saturday; afternoon Sunday, May–September. Closed national and tribal holidays. Donations accepted.

Exhibits in the museum include both Navajo artifacts and prehistoric Anasazi artifacts. Group tours can be arranged by appointment.

Betatakin is one of three well-preserved Anasazi cliff dwellings in Navajo National Monument. National Park Service photo by Natt N. Dodge.

A view in the Keet Seel Ruin, Navajo National Monument. National Park Service photo by Fred E. Mang, Jr.

Inscription House Ruin, in Navajo National Monument, is not open to the public. National Park Service photo by Fred E. Mang, Jr.

Betatakin Ruin, in Navajo National Monument. National Park Service photo
by Fred E. Mang, Jr.

Kachinas

When the Spanish invaders arrived in the Southwest in 1540, every Indian pueblo except one had what the Hopis called kachinas. These were men, costumed, masked, and painted with elaborate symbolism, who participated in ceremonies in the village plazas or in the kivas. They represented supernatural spirits that were themselves called kachinas, and the dancers were believed to have supernatural powers. Some of the dancers were very earthy clowns. Others were impersonators of spirits both good and evil. Occasionally paintings of kachinas were made on the walls of prehistoric kivas.

To teach children all the symbolism of the costumes, and to help them learn the stories about supernatural beings, men often carved and painted wooden dolls in the form of kachinas. Today the Pueblo Indians still have kachina dancers, and they make kachina dolls for children—and for anyone interested in buying them. Archeologists sometimes find kachina dolls in excavations.

Nokachok kachina doll from the Keams Canyon area. These dolls are made by Hopi and Zuni Indians. Field Museum of Natural History photo.

NEWSPAPER ROCK PETROGLYPHS
(*See Petrified Forest National Park*)

OLD ORAIBI
(oh-RYE-bee)

From Tuba City at the junction of US 164 and Arizona 264, drive southeast 50 miles on Arizona 264. Mail address: Hopi Indian Agency, Keams Canyon, AZ 86034. Phone: 602/738-2228. Visitors are asked to check in at the Community Building. Photography only with permission. Camping nearby. Open free daily.

Old Oraibi has been inhabited continuously since A.D. 1100. When scientists were working out a way to date ruins by studying tree rings, some of the most important information came from the wooden beams in ancient buildings in Oraibi. Visitors should respect the desire of the Hopi people for privacy in their homes.

PAINTED ROCKS STATE PARK

Drive 13 miles west of Gila Bend on Interstate 8, then 12 miles north on access road. Mail address: Arizona State Parks, 800 W. Washington, Phoenix, AZ 85007. Phone: 602/683-2151. Open daily, all year. Admission charged.

Within the park is a group of Indian rock-art drawings of snakes, lizards, men and geometric figures. The meaning of the drawings is uncertain, but they may represent a system of record keeping.

PARK OF THE CANALS

1700 North Horne, Mesa. From AZ 360, Exit 9, drive north to Brown Road, then right to Horne. Mail address: Mesa Southwest Museum, 53 Macdonald, Mesa, AZ 85201. Phone: 602/644-2351. Open free, sunrise to sunset.

In the city park are preserved a remnant of the 500 miles of irrigation canals built by the Hohokam people throughout the Salt River Valley, where as many as 20,000 farmers once flourished. Across the park the volunteer

Southwest Archaeology Team works at excavating a Hohokam village every Saturday morning. Visitors are invited to observe and even to dig after a training session.

PETRIFIED FOREST NATIONAL PARK

From Gallup, New Mexico, drive 69 miles southwest on Interstate 40 to northern park entrance and Visitor Center. Or from Holbrook drive 19 miles southeast on US 180 to Rainbow Forest entrance and museum. Mail address: Petrified Forest National Park, AZ 86028. Phone: 602/524-6228. Park open daily. Visitor centers closed certain holidays. Admission charged.

This area, notable for its deposits of petrified wood and paleontological resources from the Triassic period, also contains over 550 archeological sites. These sites demonstrate almost continuous occupation from the Paleo-Indian through historic Navajo periods. Two of the sites are easily reached by the 28-mile park road.

The Puerco Indian Ruins, 11 miles south of the Painted Desert Visitor Center, contained about 150 rooms when it was occupied up to 600 years ago. In addition, hundreds of petroglyphs—pictures and symbols pecked into the area's sandstone boulders—are found adjacent to the ruins.

A reconstructed ruin called Agate House is located adjacent to the Long Logs Interpretive Trail in the park's Rainbow Forest District. Here the Anasazi builders used blocks of petrified wood to erect a small structure.

Another prehistoric site, Newspaper Rock, is located off the main park road one mile south of Puerco Ruins. Here, a large sandstone boulder covered with dozens of petroglyphs can be viewed from an overlook.

The Rainbow Forest Museum, near the park's southern entrance, contains several exhibits that interpret the area's prehistory.

PICTURE ROCKS RETREAT

From Interstate 10 at north edge of Tucson turn west on Ina Rd. At intersection with Wade Ave., turn left and drive about a mile to entrance. Open free, daily, during daylight hours. Inquire at office for directions to site. A short, well maintained path leads to a trail exposed rock area on which a variety of petroglyphs can be seen. The Redemptorist Fathers maintain the site and welcome visitors.

PIMERIA ALTA HISTORICAL SOCIETY MUSEUM

223 Grand Avenue, Nogales, AZ 85628. Phone: 602/287-4621. Open free, Monday–Saturday; Sunday afternoon. Closed certain holidays.

A large area of southern Arizona and northern Sonora in Mexico was once known as Pimería Alta. The story of its people from the days of the Hohokam to historic times is told in exhibits in this museum.

PUEBLO GRANDE MUSEUM

4619 E. Washington St., Phoenix, AZ 85034. Phone: 602/495-0900. Open Monday–Saturday; afternoon Sunday. Closed certain holidays. Admission charged.

Here, inside the city of Phoenix, is a large archeological site with an accompanying museum, which illuminates the life of the Hohokam from about A.D. 500 to 1400. Trails with explanatory signs lead to a large platform structure—a mound built of earth—upon which small buildings once rested. They may have served cer-

Petroglyphs in Petrified Forest National Park. National Park Service photo by George A. Grant.

Petroglyphs made by Indians long ago on a sandstone cliff in Petrified Forest National Park. National Park Service photo by George A. Grant.

emonial functions and for storage of food. Around this structure is a village spread over a 2-mile diameter area.

From the mound it is possible to see remnants of irrigation canals. A whole system of canals, totaling possibly 500 miles in length, once made the Phoenix area a very productive farming region. Corn, jackbeans, lima beans, kidney beans, tepary beans, amaranth, two kinds of squash, cotton, and possibly tobacco grew well here. Besides raising crops, the Hohokam people of Pueblo Grande gathered wild plant food and hunted desert animals of many kinds. They produced beautiful pottery and other artifacts, and made ornaments of shell, imported from the Gulf of California.

Irrigation farming began about A.D. 100 in and around Phoenix. No one knows whether the Hohokam invented this practice themselves or borrowed the idea from Mexico, but as soon as water flowed onto the dry land, food increased greatly and so did population. This abundance, however, brought problems. The irrigation necessary for dependable crops may have caused the ground to become waterlogged and salt saturated.

In addition to waterlogging, other problems beset the Hohokam around Phoenix. Salt in the water damaged the walls of their buildings. Occasional floods on the Salt River destroyed the irrigation canals. Frequent floods occurred during the late 1300s. Life became increasingly difficult, and by A.D. 1450 the residents of Pueblo Grande and the surrounding area had all migrated from the Salt River Valley. Probably the Pima and the Tohono o'dham (Papago) Indians of today are descendants of the ancient Hohokam.

The Museum. Exhibits consist of materials recovered from this large site. Much of the excavation was done with the help of crews who were on work relief during the Depression. The museum building was designed after the truncated pyramids of Mexico, reflecting the influence of Mexico on the ancient Southwest. The structure incorporates sophisticated equipment and research laboratories, which will contribute to continuing investigation of the Hohokam. The museum and the archeological site are maintained by the city of Phoenix.

Special Feature. Visible here is a court in which the inhabitants may have played a ball game that was popular in prehistoric times in much of Mexico and Central America.

Passport in Time

Responding to the growing interest of the public in archeology, the Forest Service of the Department of Agriculture has developed a program in which people may take part as volunteers. Called Passport in Time (or PIT), the program is spreading to national forests throughout the United States.

Passport in Time makes it possible for volunteers to work under professional supervision in actual digs and in a variety of other archeological activities. For information apply to Passport in Time Clearinghouse, P.O. Box 18364, Washington, D.C. Phone: 202/293-0922.

This logo is used to indicate a World Heritage Site.

SHARLOT HALL MUSEUM
(SHAR-lot)

415 West Gurley, Prescott, AZ 86301. Phone: 602/445-3122. Open free, Tuesday—Saturday; afternoon Sunday. Closed holidays except Memorial Day, Independence Day and Labor Day.

One room in this museum is devoted to prehistoric cultural material from Arizona, particularly from the area around Prescott.

SMOKI MUSEUM
(smoke-eye)

126 North Arizona St., Prescott, AZ 86301. Phone: 602/445-1230. Open free, June—September, weekdays except Wednesday; winter by appointment.

A group of non-Indians, calling themselves the Smoki, have devoted a great deal of energy to the study and preservation of Native American cultures in the Southwest. They have gathered in this small museum some prehistoric Arizona artifacts, together with ethnological material.

SUNSET CRATER NATIONAL MONUMENT

From Flagstaff drive 15 miles north-east on US 89, then follow directional signs on the paved loop road. Mail address: 2717 North Steves Blvd., Flagstaff, AZ 86004. Phone: 602/427-7040. Visitor Center open daily. Closed certain holidays. Admission charged. Camping.

Although archeological sites that have been excavated here are not visitable, Sunset Crater is of archeological interest because of the volcanic eruptions that took place between the growing seasons of A.D. 1064 and 1065. Indians who followed the Sinagua way of life, living in pithouses in the vicinity of the volcano, moved to the southern margin of the cinder fall where they resumed farming. A little later a group of the Sinagua people moved to the cinder-covered Wupatki area and began farming there. The stone pueblos they built can be seen in Wupatki National Monument.

Artifacts made by the Salado people at Tonto National Monument. National Park Service photo.

THREE TURKEY RUIN TRIBAL PARK

From Chinle, at the edge of Canyon de Chelly National Monument, drive south 5 miles on Arizona 7 to directional sign, then 5 miles west on a primitive road to the Three Turkey Overlook. Open free, daily, except in bad weather.

This Anasazi site was occupied for only a little more than 50 years, apparently by people who came from Mesa Verde at about the time that area was being abandoned. The ruin can be viewed from the overlook and is accessible by a hiking trail into the canyon.

TONTO NATIONAL MONUMENT

From Globe drive 4 miles west on US 60, then 28 miles northwest on Arizona 88 to the monument entrance, then 1 mile to the Visitor Center. Mail address: Box 707, Roosevelt, AZ 85545. Phone: 602/467-2241. Open daily. Closed certain holidays. Admission charged. Camping nearby.

Visits to the Upper Ruin can be made only by guided tours, October–April, which must be arranged four days in advance.

On a self-guided tour to the Lower Ruin, which closes at 5:20 p.m. in summer and at 4:20 p.m. in winter, visitors follow a trail to cliff dwellings in which people lived 600 years ago. These ruins are particularly interesting for the richness of the details they have revealed about the lives of those who inhabited them.

The Story. At about A.D. 1100, farming people from the north and east moved into Tonto Basin—the area around Tonto Creek, which flows into the Salt River. Here they lived peacefully with the Hohokam, who already farmed on irrigated land along the stream. The newcomers and the old-timers quickly learned from each other, and the result was vigorous development. Pottery-making flourished. Expert weavers made cloth in intricate patterns, with fancy designs of colored stripes, and they used some dyes not found anywhere else.

For some reason, perhaps for defense, some of the people moved from

These dwellings in Tonto National
Monument were built in the middle
of the fourteenth century. National
Park Service photos.

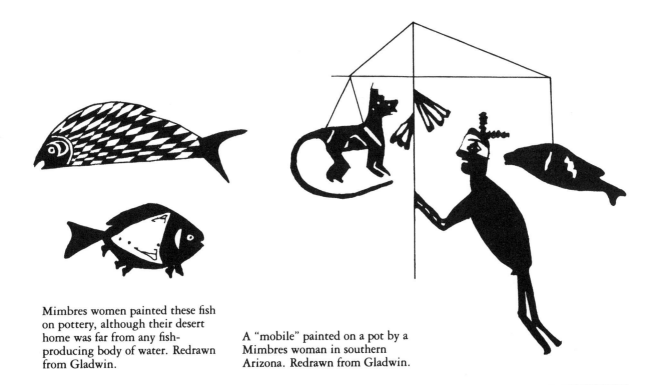

Mimbres women painted these fish on pottery, although their desert home was far from any fish-producing body of water. Redrawn from Gladwin.

A "mobile" painted on a pot by a Mimbres woman in southern Arizona. Redrawn from Gladwin.

the lower land about the year 1300. They built dwellings in several caves in the cliff, using chunks of very hard rock, which they embedded in mortar of adobe clay. The outside was then plastered with clay to give a smooth finish. The cliff villages were lived in for only about 50 years, and then inhabitants moved away—no one knows where or why.

The unique lifeway of these people, and especially their pottery style, extended over much of the valley of the Salt River, and so archeologists have called them the Salado (sah-LAH-doh), the Spanish word for salty.

The Museum. At the Visitor Center can be seen many of the things that the Salado people made and used—pottery, beautiful cloth, tools, and weapons.

Special Feature. Those who lived here apparently remodeled their houses during cold weather, when farming was over. In several places the wet clay they used to plaster the walls shows clear imprints, at shoulder height, of the fabrics in clothes worn for warmth.

TOPOC MAZE
National Register of Historic Places

From Needles, in California, drive south on Interstate 40 to Park Moabi exit, then west one half mile on a gravel road to its end. There turn left on a second gravel road; at the Y keep left, then left again 200 yards to a parking lot.

This curious huge artifact consists of parallel rows of gravel, which prehistoric people scraped into heaps a few inches high, forming paths three to four feet apart. Some of the paths cross each other although they do not form a real maze. They originally covered about 18 acres, almost half of which have been vandalized.

The meaning of the lines can only be guessed. Some archeologists think they may have been made by people who shared the later Mojave Indian belief in the need for running along certain paths as part of a purification rite.

TUSAYAN RUIN
(*See Grand Canyon National Park*)

At Tuzigoot National Monument the ancient town covered a ridge that rose 120 feet above the floor of the Verde Valley. In places the building was two stories high. National Park Service photo by Paul V. Long, Jr.

TUZIGOOT NATIONAL MONUMENT
(TOO-zee-goot)

From Flagstaff drive 49 miles southwest on US 89A to Cottonwood, then 3 miles northwest to Monument entrance. Mail address: P.O. Box 68, Clarkdale, AZ 86324. Phone: 602/634-5564. Open daily. Admission charged.

Visitors follow a trail on a self-guided tour of this prehistoric hilltop town, which once consisted of nearly a hundred rooms.

The Story. The earliest settlers of Tuzigoot were related to the Hohokam farmers, who lived more than a thousand years ago near Phoenix. Later, about A.D. 1125, they were joined by people called Sinagua, who also settled at Montezuma Castle. The newcomers, and others who arrived later, built a village of stone houses along a ridge, with a square, two-story structure on the hilltop. The village flourished and grew until the 1400s, when for some unknown reason it was abandoned. Perhaps there was an epidemic, or the land may have ceased to

be productive. Archeologists think that some of the people migrated northward, because modern Hopi and Zuni legends say that some of their families came from the neighborhood of Tuzigoot.

The Museum. Here are displays of artifacts recovered during the excavation of the site.

The Name. Tuzigoot comes from a modern Apache word meaning "crooked water," referring to Peck's Lake, an oxbow lake caused by a meander in the nearby Verde River, which winds back and forth through the valley.

UNIVERSITY OF ARIZONA, ARIZONA STATE MUSEUM

On the campus, N. Park Ave. at University Blvd., Tucson, AZ 85721. Phone: 602/621-6281. Open free, Monday–Saturday; afternoon Sunday. Closed certain holidays.

This remarkable museum has exhibits that illuminate the life of Paleo-Indian hunters of 10,000 years ago and of the Hohokam and Mogollon cul-

On the ridge in the distance stand the ruins of a village in what is now Tuzigoot National Monument. National Park Service photo by Parker Hamilton.

tures dating from A.D. 1 to 1450. Displays include artifacts from Ventana Cave, which was occupied for almost 10,000 years, and from the Naco and Lehner Paleo sites.

The latter site was discovered when a rancher in the San Pedro Valley saw some large bones exposed in an arroyo. He reported the find to Emil Haury of the Arizona State Museum. Haury excavated and found evidence that hunters, more than 10,000 years ago, killed nine mammoths and roasted some of the meat nearby.

Artifacts from the Hohokam site at Snaketown give insight into the subsistence living, clothing, housing and daily life of these desert farmers. Another exhibit explores the use of rock shelters by human beings and features a life-size replica of a Mogollon cliff dwelling.

In another exhibit are mammoth bones and the tools of mammoth hunters exactly as archeologists found them in the earth.

Temporary exhibits feature special collections and research topics by members of the museum staff.

The museum also has a rich collection of materials from the Native American tribes that have lived in Arizona in historic times.

WALNUT CANYON NATIONAL MONUMENT

From Flagstaff drive 7.5 miles east on Interstate 40 to directional sign, then 3 miles southeast to Visitor Center. Mail address: Walnut Canyon Rd., Flagstaff, AZ 86004-9705. Phone: 602/526-0571 or 3367. Open daily. Closed certain holidays. Admission charged.

Visitors can take a self-guided tour along the rim of Walnut Canyon, then down to 25 cliff-dwelling rooms. From the trail about 100 other dwellings can be seen.

The Story. Very few people seem to have lived in this beautiful spot before the eruption in A.D. 1065 of Sunset Crater, a volcano about 15 miles to the north, near present-day Wupatki National Monument. Fifty or sixty years later groups of farmers called Sinagua moved into Walnut Canyon and built

their stone houses in recesses in the cliffs. Here they lived for almost 200 years. Then, like their neighbors in this part of Arizona, they abandoned their homes and moved elsewhere. Possibly some of their descendants are now members of Pueblo Indian groups.

Special Feature. In addition to the cliff house, visitors can see a pithouse, which shows a way of life that was common before people began to build multiple dwellings of stone in the canyon.

Wupatki. About 20 years after the eruption of a nearby volcano, now called Sunset Crater, Sinagua people built a village here and began to plant crops in soil that was mulched by volcanic ash. National Park Service photo by George A. Grant.

WALPI
(WAHL-pee)

Walpi is a Hopi Indian village, built on top of a high mesa. Some of the dwellings go back at least to 1680, and remains of prehistoric houses lie on the slopes below the present village. They are not open to exploration by visitors. No photographing is allowed in Walpi, and visitors are requested not to enter private homes. *Special Feature.* Visitors may see at Walpi the Snake Dance ceremony, in the late summer of odd-numbered years. This ceremony had its origin in prehistoric times. Information about the exact date and the place where the dance is held in even-numbered years may be obtained at the Hopi Indian Agency, Keams Canyon, or at Tribal Headquarters, Kykotsmovi.

From Keams Canyon on Arizona 264 drive 11 miles west, then north at directional sign. Mail address: Hopi Indian Agency, Keams Canyon, AZ 86034. Phone: 602/738-2228. Camping nearby.

WUPATKI NATIONAL MONUMENT
(woo-POT-key)

From Flagstaff drive 32 miles north on US 89 to the Wupatki–Sunset Crater Loop Rd. entrance, then 14 miles east to the Visitor Center. Mail address: Wupatki and Sunset Crater National Monuments, 2717 N. Steves Blvd., Flagstaff, AZ 86004. Phone: 602/427-7040. Open daily, all year. Closed certain holidays. Admission charged. Camping in a nearby Forest Service campground, May–Sept.

There are about 800 ruins in the monument, nearly 100 of them within an area of one square mile. Visitors can take self-guided tours to the largest site, Wupatki, which has been partially excavated, and to one called the Citadel, which has not been excavated. At Wupatki archeologists have uncovered an ancient ball court, one of several in northern Arizona.

The Story. In A.D. 1064 a great volcano exploded and formed what is now called Sunset Crater. Volcanic cinders spread over 800 square miles. Instead

Ball Courts

The Spanish who came to Mexico and Central America in the sixteenth century saw Indians playing a game with a solid rubber ball that weighed about five pounds. The players, divided into teams, tried to keep the ball in the air and scored points by bouncing it off the sloping side walls of a specially built court. The biggest score in the game seems to have been made when a player bounced the ball through the hole in one of the doughnut-shaped stone rings that were fixed high in the wall on either side of the court. Players were forbidden to hit the ball with their hands or feet. They could direct it only with blows from their hips or knees or elbows. Apparently the game had ceremonial significance, although it is not known exactly what this was.

In Arizona archeologists have found in Hohokam settlements a number of large areas of hard-packed earth with sloping side walls which somewhat resemble the ball courts of Mexico and Central America. Excavation near one of the Arizona courts turned up a large ball similar to those used in Mexico.

---

of devastating the land, the cinders formed a kind of mulch, which may have conserved moisture, kept the ground warm, and so somewhat prolonged the growing season. This may have encouraged the Sinagua people to move into the area north of the volcano. Increased rainfall probably helped to make their new farms successful.

At one time archeologists thought that the Sinagua led a rush of Mogollon and Anasazi settlers to exploit this productive land. Artifacts and architecture characteristic of various peoples seemed to indicate that Wupatki became a sort of melting pot. Recent opinion, however, is that the Sinagua became great traders and that it was trade, not immigration that accounts for the traits that had been thought to show a mixture in population. One structure, the idea for which was certainly imported, was the circular ball court of the kind usually found much farther south and originally brought from Mexico.

People remained at Wupatki for about 150 years. Perhaps by then the land was exhausted. For whatever reason, the last inhabitants left about A.D. 1225.

The Museum. Exhibits here show methods that prehistoric Indians used in making artifacts.

The Name. Wupatki, a Hopi Indian word, means "tall house." It refers to a multi-story dwelling which, during the 1100s, had more than 100 rooms, housing perhaps 150 people.

Special Feature. Eighteen miles from Wupatki National Monument headquarters, by the Loop Road, is Sunset Crater National Monument. Here may be seen the dead mouth of the volcano that spewed out cinders to cover the surrounding area.

Pot Hound and Grave Robber

A rock hound is a collector of rocks and minerals and harms no one. A pot hound is a collector of pots and other prehistoric Indian artifacts and harms everyone. Usually a pot hound is a grave robber, because Native Americans often buried their honored dead with beautiful vessels as well as ornaments and tools. Whether or not graves are desecrated, the pot hunter is always a vandal, and a collector who buys artifacts from a pot hunter encourages vandalism which destroys forever information that may help us understand other human beings.

Amateur archeologists rightly object to pot hunters, but amateurs and professionals are no better than vandals if they dig without keeping careful, complete records of everything they do and find. Each object, no matter how seemingly insignificant, that is encountered in the ground should be recorded fully, so that all relevant detail will be available when needed.

Collecting artifacts from the surface of privately owned land is not illegal if the landowner gives permission, but such collecting can be harmful from a scientific point of view. Clues on the surface may lead to important evidence beneath the surface. The best thing an amateur can do when he or she finds any ancient object anywhere is to notify a museum or the state archeologist, giving as much exact information as possible about what was found and where. Artifacts left in place can be useful. The same objects moved can be useless.

Pot hunting—grave robbing—on public land has been forbidden since 1906 by the federal Antiquities Act. In addition many states have had their own laws to protect cultural resources. In 1979 a new federal law with more teeth was passed. It is the Archeological Resources Protection Act, which provides that pot hunters can be imprisoned for up to ten years and fined up to $10,000. In the single year in which the law was passed, government agencies estimated that more damage was done to ancient sites than had been done in the preceding 600 years. In spite of the law, and successful prosecutions under it, vandalism still continues.

Another recent law affecting archeological material is the Native American Graves and Repatriation Act, passed in 1990. Under this act skeletal remains and religious objects must be returned to the tribes to whom they rightfully belong. This act has required changes in many museum exhibits and is a reflection of increased sensitivity to the concerns of Native Americans.

A. Some of the pots that came out of
excavations on Wetherill Mesa in
Mesa Verde National Park. National
Park Service photo by Fred Mang.
B. Mogollon people who lived in the
Mimbres Valley, in southwestern
New Mexico, decorated their pottery
imaginatively with figures of animals
and human beings. C. An Anasazi
woman made this bowl about 700
years ago. Original in the museum at
Mesa Verde National Park. D. An
unusual black and white jar found at
Mesa Verde. Original in the
Colorado History Museum in
Denver. E. A Mogollon pottery
canteen made in the Tularosa style in
Arizona about A.D. 1200. Original
in the Southwest Museum, Los
Angeles.

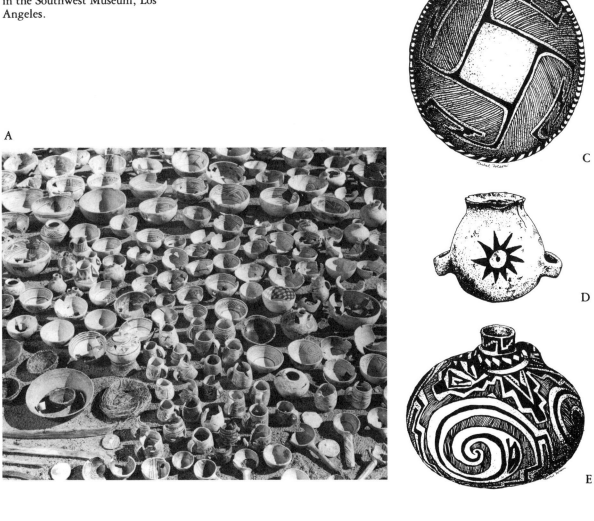

A

B

C

D

E

Colorado (southwestern)

For additional Colorado listings see Great Plains

ANASAZI HERITAGE CENTER

Three miles west of Dolores on Colorado 184. Mail address: 27501, Highway 184, Dolores, CO 81323. Phone: 303/882-4811. Open free, daily, April 15–October 31; call for schedule for the remainder of the year. Closed certain holidays.

This large museum was built by the Bureau of Land Management to house almost 2,000,000 artifacts that came from excavations called the Dolores Project that preceded the construction of nearby McPhee Dam and Reservoir. The exhibits reveal Anasazi history by tracing changes in technology, architecture and land use patterns. They also illustrate farming methods, food preparation, crafts and trade. Hands-on exhibits give visitors a chance to weave and grind corn in the Anasazi

ANASAZI NATIONAL PARK

It was the largest government-funded archeological project in U.S. history.

The Dolores Project employed 500 people to excavate the 120 sites that produced the materials to be seen here.

As this book went to press the Park Service was considering plans to create a large new national park northwest of Cortez to include a great number of sites in the area.

For information about how plans for this new park are progressing, inquire at the Cortez CU Center or at Mesa Verde National Park (see below).

CANYON PINTADO HISTORIC DISTRICT

National Register of Historic Places

From the junction of Colorado 64 and 139 near Rangely, drive south 2 miles on Colorado 139. Mail address: Bureau of Land Management, P.O. Box 928, Meeker, CO 81641. Phone: 303/878-3601. Open free, all year. Camping.

In this canyon, which has been occupied for 11,000 years, are 30 examples of rock art left by Fremont people who lived here from A.D. 600 to 1300. The first Europeans to see this art were Fathers Dominguez and Escalante who traveled through the area in 1776.

CENTER OF SOUTHWEST STUDIES

Fort Lewis College, Durango, CO 81301. On the campus, third floor of the library. Phone: 303/247-7210. Open free, afternoons Monday–Friday. Closed certain holidays.

In a display area there are exhibits of Anasazi pottery and other artifacts, together with modern Indian rugs and baskets.

This museum also preserves a collection of ceramics from the Yellow Jacket area in southwestern Colorado.

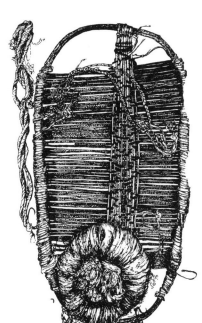

Basketmaker mothers carried babies in cradles made of fiber. The child's head rested on the round pillow, and a pad of soft, shredded cedar bark served as a diaper. After a Mesa Verde photo by Faha.

Classifying the Anasazi Cultures

The culture of the Anasazi people in the Southwest developed in rather clearly defined stages. You will often find these stages referred to according to what is called the Pecos Classification, a set of names agreed to at Pecos, NM in 1927. Here it is:

pre-A.D. 1	Basketmaker I
A.D. 1 to 500	Basketmaker II
A.D. 450 to 750	Basketmaker III
A.D. 750 to 900	Pueblo I
A.D. 800/850 to 1100	Pueblo II
A.D. 1100 to 1300	Pueblo III
A.D. 1300 to 1700	Pueblo IV
A.D. 1700 to the present	Pueblo V

CHIMNEY ROCK

Reached by an access road off Colorado 151 west of Pagosa Springs. Open free, during the summer, only to guided tours. The ruins are not accessible without a guide. Tours are conducted daily between May 15 and September 15 each year. Groups larger than 7 persons should make reservations; smaller groups may attend tours without prior notice. Visitors should contact the San Juan National Forest, Pagosa Ranger District, P.O. Box 310, Pagosa Springs, CO 81147 or phone: 303/264-2268 to make reservations and to confirm tour schedules. The number and timing of tours may vary during a season. The tour enters a protective peregrine falcon habitat closure on two half-mile trails. One trail is moderately challenging, the other is an easy walk. Wheelchair facilities are under construction: contact the Pagosa District for more information about barrier-free access.

Here, a thousand feet above the valley floor, on a ridge with a magnificent view in all directions, perhaps as many as 500 Anasazi people lived between A.D. 925 and 1125. The population of neighboring related villages may have been 1500. Archeologists believe that a colony of male priests from Chaco Canyon, 90 miles away joined this community about A.D. 1076 and found wives among the resident villagers. After the colonists arrived, in the spring or fall of the year, construction was begun on a Chacoan Great House and kiva. The building was laid out carefully in an L shape, with the kiva to one side of a block of rooms. Tons of rock were then brought in to be chipped and fitted together in fine, even courses.

A great deal of archeological detective work recently done in the Southwest makes this Chimney Rock scenario likely. It is clear that the colonists came from Chaco Canyon, because the construction of new buildings at the site is typical of Chaco towns. The place was laid out according to a predetermined plan characteristic of Chaco, and the beautiful masonry was Chacoan, much finer than that of local buildings near by. The details of the kiva could only have been engineered by peo-

The Bureau of Land Management-Anasazi Heritage Center is located just downhill from Escalante Ruin, a 12th-century Anasazi site, and adjacent to McPhee Reservoir. Bureau of Reclamation photo by Joan Fleetman.

ple—most likely priests—who were familiar with religious architecture. The pottery that was found at the site gives evidence of intermarriage with local women. None of it was made in the Chacoan style. Since women in Pueblo societies were traditionally the potters, it is safe to assume that women did not accompany the colonists from Chaco.

The unusual, even improbable, location for the town, high above the valley and, during the summer months, a mile or more from the nearest drinking water, may have been chosen for religious reasons. Ample snow decreased the water problem in late fall and winter, and this leads to the idea that building must have been done in fall or spring, when water for making mud mortar and plaster did not have to be carried in jars uphill from valley streams. Additional evidence for the religious aspect of the prehistoric Chimney Rock settlement is a historic Taos Indian legend. The two spectacular pinnacles, or chimneys, which rise beside the site were supposedly dedi-cated to deities known as the Twin War Gods.

A recently discovered connection between the Chaco Great House and an astronomical phenomenon called the northern lunar standstill shows that Chimney Rock may have been an important Chaco ceremonial site. Every 18.6 years, the full moon rises exactly between the twin pinnacles of Chimney rock, as viewed from the Great House, and the dates of this striking moonrise coincide with the construction dates of the Great House: A.D. 1076 and 1094. Chaco priests and worshippers may have made pilgrimages from Chaco Canyon to visit Chimney Rock during these standstill years.

The Chimney Rock community was one of a number of outliers or colonies related to the large center in Chaco Canyon (see New Mexico listing). Among other outliers were the Salmon Ruin, in New Mexico, and the Dominguez and Escalante Ruins, in Colorado. The motivation for the colonies is still not fully understood. Some ar-cheologists believe they were established to encourage production of resources for the center. Others think they may have served to relieve over-population at the center.

COLORADO NATIONAL MONUMENT

Four miles from Grand Junction via Hwy. 340 and Monument Road. Mail address: Fruita, CO 81521. Visitor Center open daily, all year. Admission charged in summer.

A panel in the Visitor Center gives information about the Fremont culture and displays some artifacts.

People sharing the Chaco culture built rooms and circular kivas a thousand feet above the surrounding valley here at Chimney Rock, in Colorado. Photo by Frank W. Eddy.

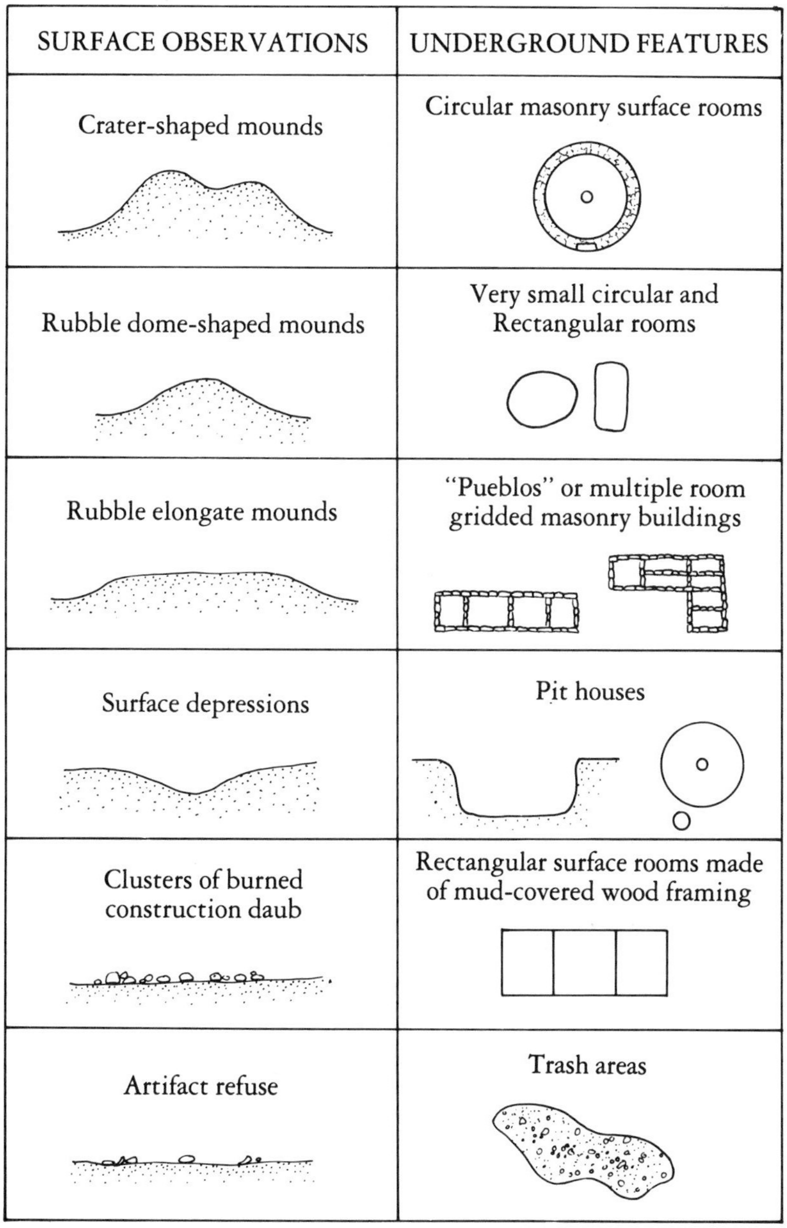

SURFACE OBSERVATIONS	UNDERGROUND FEATURES
Crater-shaped mounds	Circular masonry surface rooms
Rubble dome-shaped mounds	Very small circular and Rectangular rooms
Rubble elongate mounds	"Pueblos" or multiple room gridded masonry buildings
Surface depressions	Pit houses
Clusters of burned construction daub	Rectangular surface rooms made of mud-covered wood framing
Artifact refuse	Trash areas

Redrawn from *Archaeological Investigations at Chimney Rock Mesa: 1970–1972,* by Frank W. Eddy. Boulder, Colorado Archeological Society, 1977.

Surface Surveys

When archeologists walk over an area, they often find evidence that tells them what lies below the surface. This diagram shows (left) features of the kind found on the surface near Chimney Rock and (right) what lay hidden in the ground below.

Right, and opposite: Excavation and stabilization of the Great Kiva in the Escalante portion of Dominguez and Escalante Ruins.

THE CORTEZ CU CENTER

25 North Market, P.O. Box 1326, Cortez, CO 81321. Phone: 303/565-1151. Open free, daily during summer months and on a part time scheudle in other months.

The museum, with the cooperation of the University of Colorado and the Cortez community, has exhibits from the Anasazi Heritage Center, the Ute Mountain Ute Park and the Yellow Jacket site. It also has displays on the archeology that has been done by the University of Colorado.

Special Feature. Commercially operated tours to the many archeological sites in the area originate here. The tours include visits to any digs in progress. Professional guides at each site give talks.

CROW CANYON ARCHAEOLOGICAL CENTER

From Cortez drive north on US 666, then left on County Road L, then south on County Road 23—a total distance of four miles. Mail address: 23390 County Road K, Cortez, CO 81321. Phone: 303/565-8975. Open free, summer months.

This very active educational institution operates a variety of hands-on programs open to the public for various fees. One week-long program is designed for high school students who want to do actual excavating. Full information about the programs can be obtained by writing or phoning the Center. When excavation is in progress at an Anasazi site known as Sand Canyon Pueblo, visitors are invited to come and observe. There is a self-guided tour.

CURECANTI NATIONAL RECREATION AREA, NATIONAL PARK SERVICE

From Gunnison drive 16 miles west on US 50 to entrance and Visitor Center. Mail address: 102 Elk Creek, Gunnison, CO 81230. Phone: 303/641-2337, or 0406. Open free, daily, early June to end of September. Camping.

Surveys and excavation here have led to some unusual finds. Sites in the area

show continued re-occupation for an enormously long period—the earliest with a Carbon-14 date of 10,100 before the present, the most recent about A.D. 1500. Obviously the resources along the nearby banks of the Gunnison River (now partially flooded by a dam) brought people back time after time. But what were the special attractions of the place? Archeologists are not quite sure.

Another intriguing puzzle has been the discovery of several kinds of structure made of poles and mud—a method known as wattle and daub. These have been dated at the Archaic period (between 6000 and 4000 years ago), but exactly what kind of structure they were has not been determined.

At a site more than 200 miles north and east of Curecanti similar structures were unearthed in 1981 by salvage archeologists and dated at about 8000 years ago, amazingly early for wattle and daub.

Testing, excavation, and study of Curecanti will be ongoing, and visitors are welcome to watch the work. Interpretive displays in the Visitor Center give an idea of discoveries at

the site, and some days of the week a guide will lead interpretive walks. For information about dates and hours of walks, phone the Visitor Center.

DINOSAUR NATIONAL MONUMENT

From Jensen, Utah, on US 40, drive north 7 miles on Utah 149 to Visitor Center. Mail address: P.O. Box 210, Dinosaur, CO 81610. Phone: 303/374-2216. Open daily, all year. Admission charged. Camping.

Prehistoric people may have been in this area as early as 11,000 years ago, although archeological excavation has revealed few details about them. Fremont people made their homes from 100 B.C. to A.D. 1200 along rivers and creeks, hunting, gathering and farming in the monument area. Their petroglyphs (rock carvings) and pictographs (rock paintings) may be seen in several places. The best and most accessible are east of the dinosaur quarry on a monument road. For information about their location, inquire at Dinosaur Quarry Visitor Center.

More recently, Ute Indians lived in one part of the monument area, Shoshone Indians in another, known as Browns Park. Descendants of the Utes now occupy a reservation nearby.

DOMINGUEZ AND ESCALANTE RUINS

From Dolores drive 3 miles west on Colorado 184 to the site entrance marker adjacent to the Anasazi Heritage Center. Mail address: 27501 Hwy. 184, Dolores, CO 81323. Phone: 303/882-4811. Open free, daily, all year. Closed certain holidays.

This Anasazi site intrigues archeologists because it seems to have been occupied simultaneously by people from two different cultural backgrounds. On top of a hill are the ruins, called Escalante, of a large, pre-planned village, built in the style of Chaco Canyon, in New Mexico. Dominguez, downhill from Escalante, is one of half a dozen small, rather simple sites in the neighborhood, built in the tradition of Mesa Verde, which is much closer by.

Shifting sands at Great Sand Dunes National Monument sometimes reveal artifacts and campsites buried as long as 10,000 years ago. National Park Service photo by Robert Haugen.

Some archeologists believe that colonists from Chaco came here as traders in the late eleventh century and built their four-sided village of large masonry rooms surrounding a ceremonial kiva, with another kiva just outside the walls. Since few articles of trade were discovered in the excavation, another theory is that the Chacoans may have moved here because the population had increased too much at home.

Dominguez Ruin consists of a kiva and four rooms, one of which was small and not very well constructed. These dwellings seem to have been occupied by no more than two or three families. Yet excavation of one room in the modest site revealed the burial of a woman, together with grave goods of extraordinary quality and quantity. Among other things were three elaborate pendants, turquoise and shell mosaics, ceramic vessels, and thousands of beads made from turquoise, jet, and shell. Burials of this sort were not characteristic of Mesa Verde people. Is it possible that a woman of wealth and high rank from Escalante was buried at more humble Dominguez? If so, guez.

The Name. In 1776 two Franciscan explorers, Father Dominguez and Father Escalante, set up camp near the present town of Dolores. Dominguez was ill, and while he rested Escalante climbed a hill and came upon the ruin which, he said, "was . . . of the same form as those of the Indians of New Mexico." The site was later named for him, and in 1976 the neighboring site was named for his partner, Dominguez.

The large-scale interaction—here and elsewhere in the region—between Mesa Verde people and those of Chaco Canyon is still not entirely clear, and archeologists hope that the study of Dominguez and Escalante Ruins will lead to solving some of the puzzles.

what were the other relationships between the two different peoples? Perhaps the Chacoans brought to the area more elaborate religious and social patterns than the indigenous people were used to, and they in turn provided the Chacoans with surplus food or other things that could have been taken back to Chaco Canyon to supply the people there.

GREAT SAND DUNES NATIONAL MONUMENT

From Alamosa drive 14 miles north on Colorado 17, then 18 miles east on 6 Mile Lane to Visitor Center. Mail address: Great Sand Dunes National Monument, Mosca, CO 81146. Phone: 719/378-2312. Open at all times. Admission charged. Camping.

People have been leaving tools and weapons around the Sand Dunes for 10,000 years. Two archeological sites in the area have revealed the campgrounds of people who hunted giant bison, which are now extinct. Bones of the animals have been excavated together with special spear points that Paleo-Indians used when they hunted these huge animals. Points of this kind were first found near Folsom, New Mexico, and are called Folsom points. Later, hunters, belonging to various groups including some Pueblo Indians, followed great herds of bison, antelope, deer and elk which roamed the San Luis Valley near the Sand Dunes. Archeologists have discovered indications that whole families traveled along definite routes on these

The painted kiva, Lowry Pueblo Ruins, as it once appeared.

hunting expeditions from the south into the valley.

Special Feature. Winds blowing across the San Luis Valley for thousands of years deposited sand at the foot of the mountains along the valley's eastern side, forming some of the world's highest dunes. Hiking is allowed on the dunes, which shift constantly and from time to time uncover a spot where Indians once lived and left artifacts. Visitors may look at but not loot such sites.

One of the authors of this book has written a mystery-adventure story for young readers that tells of the discovery of an archeological site here. The book *Sand Dune Pony* by Troy Nesbit (pseud.) is available at Monument headquarters.

HOVENWEEP NATIONAL MONUMENT
(See Utah)

LOWRY PUEBLO RUINS

From Cortez drive north 18 miles on US 666 to Pleasant View, then 9 miles west on a gravel road. Mail address: Bureau of Land Management, Federal Building, 701 Camino Del Rio, Durango, CO 81301. Phone: 303/247-4082. Open free, at all times.

About A.D. 850, possibly earlier, people began to garden at this site. Then for some reason the village was abandoned. Around 1090 it was reoccupied, and eventually it grew to be a community of 40 rooms, in part three stories high, with eight small kivas in addition to a great kiva. In the next 30 years villagers repeatedly altered, rebuilt and added to their dwellings. They filled old rooms with trash and constructed new ones adjoining. The last remodeling was done by masons whose stonework was different from that of earlier builders. Possibly they were newcomers from Chaco Canyon. Soon they, too, deserted the pueblo for what reason archeologists have not determined. People may have left because the land was not able to support the increased population. They seem to have moved without pressure from hostile invaders or from any catastrophe such as fire or drought.

Special Feature. During their first 20 years at the site, villagers built a kiva with a plastered wall on which they painted designs. At least four subsequent coats of plaster were added and decorated. Later this ceremonial room was filled in and a new one built on top of it. Archeologists discovered the painted kiva in the course of excavating the ruins, and the Bureau of Land Management, which administers the site, has built a shelter over it to protect the paintings while continuing to allow visitors to observe them. Despite (or perhaps because of) several efforts to preserve the mural in the Painted Kiva, it is almost totally gone. Only about 6 square inches of the pattern remain.

Cliff Palace, in Mesa Verde National Park, seen from about the place where two cowboys first saw it in 1888. National Park Service photo by Leland J. Abel.

Richard Wetherill (third from right in background), discoverer of Cliff Palace in Mesa Verde, sometimes conducted tourists into the area. Here he rests with some of them in Cliff Palace. National Park Service photo.

Before: When archeologists began excavation in Long House, on Wetherill Mesa, this is what it looked like. *After:* As Long House appears now, cleared of debris, walls stabilized. National Park Service photo.

MESA VERDE NATIONAL PARK
(MAY-suh VER-day)
A World Heritage Site

Midway between Cortez and Mancos on US 160 turn south to park entrance, then drive 21 miles on the park road to Headquarters and museums. Mail address: National Park Service, Mesa Verde National Park, CO 81330. Phone: 303/529-4461 or 4475. Open all year. Admission charged at park entrance. Camping, May 1 through Oct. 14, within the park, 5 miles from entrance. *Note:* The hours for tours, museum, and other visitor services are subject to change. For the latest information consult Park Headquarters.

Mesa Verde is really a huge outdoor archeological museum, which contains many different sites. The park occupies a stretch of high tableland, or mesa, which is cut by deep canyons with steep cliff walls. In many of the canyons prehistoric people found alcoves and rock shelters, and there they built some of the most beautiful and interesting villages to be found in the Southwest. On the mesa top other ruins can be visited. Because there is such

a large number of visitable sites, each with its own special interest, each will be discussed separately in the following pages. All, however, share the same general history.

The Story. At about the beginning of the fifth century A.D., people started to cultivate small gardens in the semiarid Mesa Verde area. For 800 years they lived here, improving their farming techniques, eventually building dams and storage ponds and irrigation systems. Through one stage after another they developed a special style of architecture, and their pottery took on a beauty and quality that distinguished it from other pottery made in the Southwest in prehistoric times. Now and then the women, who did the work of shaping and decorating pots, adopted new ideas or fads, and these changes in fashion were often very marked. As a result archeologists have been able to use pottery types as an aid in determining the dates of certain events in the region.

Mesa Verde was one of the three regions where Anasazi culture reached a very high point before A.D. 1276. (The others were Chaco Canyon and

Kayenta.) The year 1276 was important. At about that date people began to abandon the mesas and the canyons where they had been living. Experts disagree on the reasons for the whole-sale migration away from this ancient homeland. Some say that a 23-year-long drought set in; others believe raiders began to attack the villages, seeking the food stored there. Possibly the Mesa Verde people began to have quarrels among themselves and to develop rival factions. They may have moved to other regions because of a breakdown in the general social structure on the mesa.

For whatever reason, everyone did move away over 600 years ago, and what you see now is the evidence of achievement in a far from lush environment, over a period of eight centuries. For glimpses of the life led by descendants of the Mesa Verde people, visitors can go to present-day pueblos along the Rio Grande River and to the Hopi villages on the Hopi mesas. It was in these areas that the emigrants made their homes after they left Mesa Verde.

For a clear and detailed picture of

One of the striking architectural features of Cliff Palace, in Mesa Verde National Park, is the square tower with its t-shaped doorway in the fourth story. National Park Service photo by Fred Mang.

Mesa Verde life at each of its stages, visitors should start at the museum in Park Headquarters.

The Museum. Here well-arranged displays give an orderly and illuminating introduction to prehistoric life in the Mesa Verde area. Exhibits lead the visitor on a journey through time, beginning with the days when Basketmaker women ground corn kernels into usable cornmeal by rubbing them between a small stone called a mano and a large stone called a metate. For cooking, these women used baskets in special ways. Corn or other dry food might be placed in a broad, flat basket along with heated rocks and stirred till it was parched. Some baskets were so finely woven that they could hold water. To cook food in such a vessel, a woman dropped hot rocks into the water to make it boil.

Later at Mesa Verde women continued to weave baskets, but they also learned to make pottery. Men hunted with bows and arrows instead of depending on spears and spear-throwers as their ancestors had done. They were adept at manipulating fibers—yucca fibers, dog hair, human hair—all of

which they made into cord. Using the cord they wove sandals, bags, belts, and nets for catching game. Combining cord and strips of rabbit fur they wove blankets. (The magnificent dog-hair sashes in the museum were not found at Mesa Verde but in Obelisk Cave, in nearby northeast Arizona.)

By A.D. 600 people had begun to live in the kind of dwelling called a pithouse. This was a pit two or three feet deep, roofed over with branches and mud and entered by a ladder through a hole in the roof.

From this half-underground house, Anasazi architecture evolved in two different and fascinating ways, as an exhibit in the museum shows. Step by step, people learned to build homes of stone entirely above ground, but still with entrances through the roof. At the same time they dug deeper rooms entirely underground, and these they used as ceremonial chambers, now called kivas.

For a long time the stone houses clustered together in villages on the mesa top. Then people began to build in caves in the cliffs. For 75 or 100 years they lived in the cliff dwellings

Spruce Tree House is usually the first ruin seen by visitors to Mesa Verde National Park. National Park Service photo.

and tossed their trash down over the side. Refuse piled up, and very often it was entirely sheltered by the over-hanging rock. In the dry Southwest-ern air the refuse did not decay, and the result was that archeologists found the trash heaps a mine of relics from the past. Many of their finds can be seen in the museum.

Spruce Tree House

Open daily, summer, self-guided trip; three guided tours per day, winter.

From the museum a good trail (walking time 45 minutes to one hour) leads to the Spruce Tree House ruin in the canyon nearby.

This is an unusually good place to examine a kiva, a type of ceremonial room which was hollowed out of the rock or dug into the earth. Such un-derground chambers were common at Anasazi sites in the Southwest.

Entrance to a kiva was by ladder through a hole in the courtyard floor. This entrance hole also allowed smoke to escape from the fire, which fur-nished heat and some light. Fresh air

came down into the chamber through a ventilator shaft, built at one side. In front of the opening to the shaft inside the kiva, an upright slab of rock de-flected the incoming air and kept it from scattering ashes and smoke across the room. At intervals around the wall of the kiva stood masonry columns called pilasters.

The roof of a kiva rested on these pilasters, and it was ingeniously built. First, a row of logs, with their ends supported by the pilasters, was laid around the room. Then another row of logs was laid on top of this. In this second row the ends of each log were placed in the middle of the logs below them. On top of this second row an-other was similarly placed. The result of this cribbing was a dome-shaped structure. After the logs were all in place, they were covered with earth which was leveled off to serve as part of the courtyard floor.

In the kiva members of a clan or a society held their ceremonies. Here also they lounged and sometimes worked at their looms. Apparently it was the men and not the women who did the fine Mesa Verde weaving. In many

Ruins Road

(Two loops totaling 12 miles in length.) Open 8 a.m. to 8 p.m. in summer; closed in winter. If you follow this road, which runs along the mesa top, you will see ruins in the order in which development took place during the course of Mesa Verde history.

1. A pithouse built in the A.D. 500s.
2. Pithouses built in the A.D. 600s and 700s.
3. Pueblos built A.D. 850, 900, 950, 1000 and 1075.
4. Sun Point Pueblo, built A.D. 1100 to 1300 before people moved down into the canyon, taking with them material from the roofs and walls of their old homes to use in building new ones.
5. Sun temple, a large ceremonial center.
6. Cliff Palace. Open 9 a.m. to 7 p.m. summer; self-guided tours. Ranger-guided tours in spring and fall start at the Viewpoint on the road. (Inquire about hours at Park Head-quarters.) Total walking distance, one-

places in the Anasazi Southwest there were also great kivas, each large enough to serve a whole community.

The history of the kiva seems to be something like the following. Early people lived in semi-subterranean pit-houses. They may have conducted certain clan or society ceremonies in these dwellings. Or they may have had special large pithouses for community-wide ceremonies.

Then among the Anasazi the type of house changed. People began to build their dwellings entirely above ground. At the same time, following a conservative impulse, they continued to hold their ceremonies in the old-fashioned type of pithouse. Later apparently, they got the notion that if holding ceremonies partly underground was a good idea, it would be an even better idea to hold them in rooms that were all the way underground. So, fully subterranean kivas were built.

The archeologist at the left is using surveying instruments as he maps a site on Wetherill Mesa, in Mesa Verde National Park. Atop the tripod the photographer is recording with care every stage of the excavation of the site. National Park Service photo by Al Hayes.

Two kivas in the south courtyard in Mesa Verde's Balcony House. National Park Service photo by Jack E. Boucher.

quarter mile; time required, 45 minutes to one hour.

In this alcove and at other cliff dwellings during the 1200s, the arts of weaving and pottery making reached their peak. When Mesa Verde was abandoned, people left most of their possessions behind and the vacant dwellings were undisturbed by white settlers until one snowy winter day in 1888 when two cowboys, Richard Wetherill and Charles Mason, discovered the pueblo and named it Cliff Palace. Although many walls had tumbled and dust had filled some rooms, Wetherill and Mason found treasures of pottery and other artifacts in the ruins.

7. Viewpoints. Along Ruins Road are a number of turnouts from which it is possible to see structures of several kinds in the canyon walls. Some are small granaries, or storerooms. Others are pueblos of various sizes. One is a ceremonial site. These sites are not now accessible. To enter and leave many of them, the Mesa Verde people had to use small handholds and footholds they had chopped in the rock with hammerstones or axes made of harder rock.

8. Balcony House. Ranger-guided trips start at the Viewpoint sign in the Balcony House parking area on the hour and half-hour from 9 a.m. to 5 p.m. in summer. The total walking distance is one-half mile. The trip takes one hour.

In this village there is a second-story walkway or balcony, left intact from prehistoric times, which suggested the name for the ruin. Visitors may walk today through the courtyards, high above the canyon floor, protected by the original wall, which has been reinforced for safety. However, archeologists have found evidence in the ruins that cliff dwellings were not alway safe for those who lived in them. Skeletons of people whose bones had been broken have turned up in burials, as have crutches and splints.

9. Cedar Tree Tower. After leaving Balcony House, visitors should stop at Cedar Tree Tower on the drive back toward the park entrance. A road one-half mile long on the mesa top leads to this curious structure, which was

inhabited before people moved down into cliff dwellings.

Near the ruins is Mummy Lake, which can be reached by a short trail leading past the ruins of another small pueblo. Some archeologists think the dry basin called Mummy Lake was once an artificial reservoir. In ancient times a series of barriers or dams higher up on the mesa collected rainwater and channeled it into ditches which ultimately led into the reservoir. The water in the ditches was muddy, and to keep some of the silt out of the reservoir, the stone-age engineers who designed this facility worked out an ingenious device. They made a sharp curve near the end of the last ditch. The curve slowed the flow of water, and some of the silt settled out before the water entered the reservoir. From Mummy Lake a bypass ditch ran along the sloping mesa, carrying water several miles to the area where Park headquarters is now located.

Not all archeologists agree with this theory. Some believe that Mummy Lake was a dance plaza.

used for ceremonial purposes. From the round tower an underground passage led to a circular kiva, which is also connected to a small niche under an overhanging rounded rock.

No one knows exactly what ceremonies went on here—or elsewhere in Mesa Verde. Archeologists do know that among the Anasazi there were people who practiced healing and magical arts. A kit used by one of them has been excavated and is on display in the museum. Archeologists also know how such kits are used in modern times, for they have studied the ceremonies of present-day Pueblo Indians, some of whom are descended from Mesa Verde people. It seems likely that ancient ceremonies resembled in some ways the modern Pueblo ceremonies. If so, they expressed the desire to have all the elements of the world working together in harmony.

10. Far View Ruins. Between the park entrance and the museum, a short side road leads to this group of ruins on the mesa top. The pueblos here were

Before: This photograph, taken by one of the Wetherill brothers, probably in the early 1890s, shows Cliff Palace as it looked when Richard Wetherill and Charles Mason discovered it in 1888. Courtesy of Library, State Historical Society of Colorado.

After: Cliff Palace, in Mesa Verde National Park, as it looks today, after archeologists excavated and stabilized the structures. National Park Service photo by Jack E. Boucher.

Mug House, one of the ruins on Wetherill Mesa, Mesa Verde National Park. National Park Service photo by Fred E. Mang, Jr.

Close to Far View Ruins another group of dwellings, with a round tower next to a kiva, has been excavated.

Wetherill Mesa

This area of the park, first opened to the public in 1973, is reached by private car from the Far View Visitor Center, then by minitrain to the top of the cliff. Guided tours are offered daily, June 9 through Labor Day. Inquire about hours at Park Headquarters.

Several ruins in the Wetherill Mesa area have been excavated. One of them, which has been prepared for visitors, is Long House. Built in an enormous rock shelter, it has 150 rooms and 21 kivas. Only Cliff Palace is larger.

Pictograph Point

Hikers who register with the ranger on duty in the park office near the Chapin Mesa Museum may follow a trail to a place where Mesa Verde people made paintings on rock surfaces.

Campfire Programs. The last stop on any day in Mesa Verde should be at the campfire program in the Morefield Campground. Nightly at 9:00, from early June through Labor Day, a ranger talks on some aspect of Mesa Verde life.

The Future. The Park Service has a large site at Yucca House National Monument about 10 miles northwest of Cortez, in Montezuma Valley below Mesa Verde. When funds become available this site will be developed and open to the public.

MUSEUM OF WESTERN COLORADO

258 South Fourth St., Grand Junction, CO 81501. Phone: 303/242-0971. Open free in winter Tuesday–Saturday; in summer also open Monday. Closed certain holidays.

In addition to historic Ute material, this museum has a collection of Mimbres pots and Fremont material from both Colorado and Utah.

PAINTED HAND PUEBLO

For directions to this back-country site that can be reached year round in dry weather by vehicle and a short hike, apply to Bureau of Land Management, San Juan Resources Area, 433 N. Main St., P.O. Box 7, Monticello, UT 84535. Phone: 801/587-2141.

In this 13th century Anasazi ruin is a masonry tower that may have been part of a prehistoric communication network that used fire by night and mica or pyrite mirrors by day for signalling.

RANGELY MUSEUM

434 S. Main St., P.O. Box 131, Rangely, CO 81648. Phone: 303/675-2612. Open free (donation appreciated), daily, June–August; Friday–Sunday, April–May, September–October; afternoon, Sunday. Camping nearby.

This museum, which has a small collection of local artifacts, sponsors tours to rock art sites, including those in the Canyon Pintado Historic Dis-

Left:
Archeologists photograph artifacts in situ, meaning in exactly the situation in which they are found. Here is a bowl, broken by a fallen rock, in a cave on Wetherill Mesa, Mesa Verde National Park. National Park Service photo.

Right:
The routes used by ancient Anasazi people at Mesa Verde as they entered and left alcoves have often weathered so much they are not usable today. Here an archeologist descends into an alcove on Wetherill Mesa by rope ladder. National Park Service photo by Al Hayes.

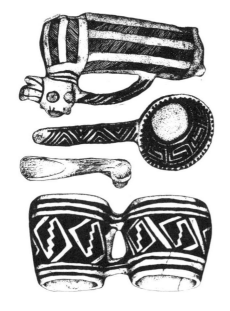

Top to bottom: Anasazi double mug. The original is in the Mesa Verde National Park museum. Mesa Verde women used the beveled edges of bone tools to scrape flesh from hides. Originals of these fleshers are in the Colorado Historical Museum, Denver. A black-on-white pottery ladle. A pot made in the shape of a duck by a woman at Mesa Verde, between A.D. 750 and A.D. 1100. The ladle and the pot are in the Mesa Verde National Park museum.

To aid in the study of prehistory, archeologists often put back together things that have been broken. On the left, a laboratory technician reconstructs a large, corrugated cooking pot found on Wetherill Mesa, in Mesa Verde National Park. On the right, the pot restored, with its yucca-fiber harness and sitting on its original doughnut-shaped rest. National Park Service photos by Fred Mang.

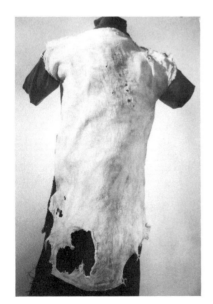

Left:
This finely woven cotton shirt was found on a mummy in Mesa Verde National Park. National Park Service photo by Fred E. Mang, Jr.

Right:
A crew of University of Colorado students digging a test trench in the trash heap beside a Pueblo II ruin on the mesa top in Mesa Verde National Park in 1968.

UTE MOUNTAIN TRIBAL PARK

Near Towaoc (TOY-ahk), 15 miles south of Cortez on US 666. Mail address: Towaoc, CO 81334. Phone: 303/565-3751, ext. 282. Tours guided by members of the Ute Tribe leave daily at 9 a.m. from the Ute Mountain Tribal Pottery Building. Those taking the tours are asked to bring their own vehicles (with plenty of gas) and to come with lunch, water, sun screen, insect repellent, and sturdy hiking boots. Fees are charged according to the length of the tour taken. Day hikes, overnight camping and backpacking can be arranged. Some roads in the park are dirt. Others are gravel surfaced.

A back-country trip in this colorful, 125,000-acre park includes visits to many surface sites, cliff dwellings, and sites of rock art. Ancient settlements here were Anasazi, similar to those adjacent in Mesa Verde National Park.

At the tribally owned Ute Mountain Pottery it is possible not only to see finished pottery for sale, but to watch the entire process of manufacture.

Special Interest. As this book went to press, newspapers reported the discovery in this immense park of a Chaco-type roadway (see Chaco Culture National Historical Park entry below).

UTE MOUNTAIN TRIBAL PARK MUSEUM

This museum, partially funded by the federal government, is scheduled to open in 1996 at the junction of US 666 and US 160 south of Cortez. In addition to exhibiting materials that illuminate Ute life of the historic period, the museum will display an extensive collection of prehistoric Anasazi perishable artifacts recovered from the Ute Mountain Tribal park. Some of this material has been turned over to the tribe by the University of Colorado Museum. For information phone 303/565-3751, ext. 282.

trict (see above). Some of the sites are of particular interest to those who seek information about archeoastronomy. The museum also sells a 24-minute video, *Rock Art of the Painted Canyon.*

SAND AND EAST ROCK CANYONS

Twelve miles west of Cortez, adjacent to Country Road G, McElmo Road. Mail address: Bureau of Land Management, San Juan Resource Area, 433 N. Main St., P.O. Box 7, Monticello, UT 84535. Phone: 801/587-2141.

Here self-guided day hikes and back-country camping trips lead to small Anasazi ruins. Minimal interpretation is provided.

Tree House Site in Johnson Canyon, Ute Mountain Tribal Park. Photo by Bob Powell; copyright by Bob Powell.

Prehistoric Cosmology

One of the intangibles that an archeologist cannot dig up is the world-view—the cosmology—of a vanished, preliterate people. However, it is sometimes possible to make an educated guess about how some ancient people saw their place in the universe. For instance, an archeologist in the Southwest can draw a number of conclusions when a small hole appears in the floor of an underground chamber that he or she calls a kiva. This hole, known as a sipapu, resembles holes found in kivas that are still in use today in Pueblo societies near the ancient ruins.

To the Hopi and other descendants of the Anasazi, a sipapu is a passageway from the underworld through which their ancestors emerged long ago. The world that people found when they came up from the underworld radiated out from a home village in six major directions. One direction was to the northeast where the sun rose on the horizon on the longest day of the year—the summer solstice. Another was to the northwest where the sun went down over the horizon on the same day. The southeasterly direction was marked by the point on the horizon over which the sun rose on the shortest day of the year, the winter solstice, and so on for the southwest. The fifth and sixth directions were straight up and straight down. With each direction certain symbols were associated—colors, animals, plants. Using these symbols, people created ceremonies, often focusing on the sun on which life depended.

From a little hole in the floor of an ancient pit, an archeologist can learn a great deal, and the same is true of other discoveries that resemble objects that have spiritual significance to Native Americans today.

Above: A jar used in kiva ceremonies. The design was painted with a brush of yucca fiber and paint made of boiled plant juices. Original is in the museum at Mesa Verde. *Below:* The ground plan of a kiva. After a drawing in the trail guide to Spruce Tree House, Mesa Verde.

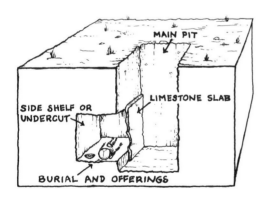

Diagram of an undercut grave at Montezuma Castle National Monument. After Schroeder and Hastings.

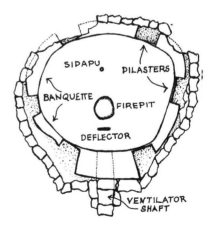

This kiva, at Casa Rinconada in Chaco Canyon, had a special entryway from an adjoining building. The woman in the foreground is standing in what was formerly a covered tunnel that led to an opening in the floor seen in the background. Photo by Julia M. Johnson; copyright by Julia M. Johnson.

Inside the Great Kiva at Aztec Ruins National Monument, after restoration. The t-shaped doorway in the center was popular in many Anasazi pueblos. The pits to the left and right may have been covered with boards and used as dance platforms or foot drums. National Park Service photo by George A. Grant.

New Mexico

ABÓ
(ah-BOH)
(Unit of Salinas Pueblo Missions National Monument)

Drive 9 miles west of Mountainair on US 60 to a directional sign, then .6 mile north on New Mexico 513. Mail address: Salinas Pueblo Missions National Monument, P.O. Box 496, Mountainair, NM 87036. Phone: 505/ 847-2400. Open free, daily, all year.

Here, in addition to a seventeenth-century Spanish mission, is an unexcavated prehistoric pueblo adjacent to an unexcavated historic pueblo. The people who lived here are recorded in historical documents as speaking the Tompiro language, which was also the language of Gran Quivira (see entry below). The Tompiro were related to the Piro who lived in the area near Socorro, New Mexico.

The pueblo, built on a pass leading into the Rio Grande valley, was a center for trade in such things as salt, hides and piñon nuts between the people of the Plains and those of the Acoma, Zuni and Santa Fe areas. After the arrival of the Spanish the prosperity of the pueblo finally declined and by 1678 the inhabitants had left to settle in other towns in the valley.

Formerly a New Mexico state monument, Abó has become part of the Salinas Pueblo Missions National Monument (see entry below). A self-guided tour leads through the site. Visitors should note that there is no drinking water at the Contact Station here.

ACOMA PUEBLO
(AH-koh-mah)

Between Albuquerque and Gallup leave Interstate 40 at Casa Blanca and drive south 14 miles on New Mexico 23. Mail address: Pueblo of Acoma, NM 87034. Phone: 505/252-1139. Open daily, all year. Closed for certain religious activities. Admission charged.

Acoma, often called Sky City, is on top of a high sandstone rock. About A.D. 900, people began to live on or near the site of the present village. Ever since A.D. 1075, the pueblo has been continuously occupied. This means that visitors at Acoma are seeing a lived-in prehistoric site, although most of the structures that are visible are obviously of recent origin.

Visitors should respect the privacy of the people of Acoma and should obtain permits from the governor of the pueblo if they wish to take photographs or do painting or drawing. The graveyards, the kivas and the waterholes are out of bounds to tourists.

AZTEC RUINS NATIONAL MONUMENT

From Farmington drive 14 miles east on US 550 to the directional marker in the town of Aztec, then one-half mile north on Ruins Road to monument entrance. Mail address: P.O. Box 640, Aztec, NM 87410. Phone: 505/ 334-6174.

This site was once a large Anasazi settlement, consisting of several multistoried Great Houses, Great Kivas, plazas and other architectural features. The West Ruin, excavated by archeologist Earl Morris, is open to the public. The sandstone masonry walls of its 500 rooms rose two and three stories high in places. A number of kivas—small round rooms—were constructed within the building itself, and in the plaza stood the Great Kiva. This has been reconstructed to show what it may have been like 800 years ago.

The design of the settlement, its fine masonry work and the Great Kiva were of the kind that originated in Chaco Canyon (see below). Aztec has long been considered by archeologists to be part of the Chaco system, which consisted of over 150 outlying settlements throughout the San Juan River basin. The West Ruin, built about A.D. 1110, first reflected the Chaco influence in architecture and pottery styles. By the mid 1100s the population diminished as the Chaco system waned. Tree-ring dating indicates a drought that caused stress throughout the region. By 1225, the population had grown again and distinct changes in architecture and pottery styles occurred. Archeologists identify this as the Mesa Verde phase of occupation at Aztec. The settlement flourished again until abandonment around A.D. 1300.

Recently, National Park Service archeologists have taken a new look at the area in and around the monument. Newly mapped sites show evidence that Aztec was a large-scale, pre-planned settlement and archeologists are beginning to reinterpret the area as "Chaco moved north," a major trade, ceremonial and administrative site that became a new center for the Anasazi. The Park Service is now involved in acquiring 290 additional acres to include these newly identified sites.

The Museum. Here are exhibits of pottery, baskets, various utensils, and tools made and used in the pueblo. Displays explain architectural features and show how the people once lived.

The Name. Early pioneers, who were much impressed by what they had heard about the Aztec Indians in Mexico, called this ruin Aztec. There is, however, no known connection between the inhabitants of this pueblo and the Aztecs, who lived in the Valley of Mexico.

Special Feature. One of the great archeologists of the Southwest, Earl Morris, who was born near Aztec, excavated this site and reconstructed the Great Kiva. When he began his careful work, he found evidence that the once-important ceremonial chamber had been used as a garbage dump before the pueblo was abandoned. Finally the roof caught fire and collapsed. Nevertheless, Morris was able to figure out details of construction and rebuild the chamber.

This screen made of reeds slid up and down over a doorway at Aztec Ruins National Monument. National Park Service photo by George A. Grant.

Opposite: The circular Great Kiva at Aztec Ruins National Monument. Although it had burned at some time long ago, enough remained so that archeologist Earl Morris could restore its interior and its outer wall. National Park Service photo.

Archeologists found this old ladder when they were excavating Aztec Ruins. National Park Service photo.

Talus House in Frijoles Canyon,
partially reconstructed, in front of
caves dug in soft rock. National Park
Service photo by A. H. White.

Artist Paul Coze's conception of life in one of the human-made caves in Frijoles Canyon. Photo by Glen Haynes, used by permission of Paul Coze.

BANDELIER NATIONAL MONUMENT
(ban-duh-LEER)

From Santa Fe drive 18 miles north on US 285 to Pojoaque (po-WAH-kay), then 17 miles west on NM 502 to NM 4, then 11 miles to monument entrance. It is 3 miles farther to the Visitor Center. Mail address: HCR 1, Box 1, Los Alamos, NM 87544. Phone: 505/672-3861. Open daily, all year except December 25. Admission charged. Camping.

This beautiful and unusual site at the bottom of a deep gorge stretches out along a little stream called Rito de los Frijoles (REE-toh day lohs free-HO-lays), Spanish for "bean creek." Along a one-mile trail visitors can see ruins of dwellings built near the cliff walls, and behind them man-made caves. In a separate section of the monument, 11 miles north of Frijoles Canyon, is an unexcavated ruin called Tsankawi (SANK-ah-WEE). Here visitors may take a self-guided tour on a two-mile trail.

The Story. People have lived in the Bandelier area for thousands of years. In Anasazi times the population increased a great deal, then at the end of the thirteenth century there was a great drought in much of the Southwest. Many Anasazi people moved from their homes, seeking water. Some of them found it here in the deep canyons that cut into the Pajarito (PAH-hah-REE-toh) Plateau. (Pajarito is Spanish for "little bird.") In the bottom of Frijoles Canyon farmers planted fields of corn, beans, and squash and built a large pueblo called Tyuonyi (chew-OHN-yee), which means "a meeting place." At the same time, some inhabitants dug storage rooms and also living quarters in the walls of the canyon. This was not too difficult because the rock is very soft—actually welded volcanic ash.

People continued to live in the canyon until the late 1500s. Then for some reason they left, as did others from various parts of the Pajarito Plateau. Today people who are probably their descendants live at the Cochiti and San

In Bandelier National Monument, three-story dwellings once stood at the base of this cliff, which is a soft rock called tuff. Builders could easily hollow it out to make storage rooms at the rear of their masonry houses. The small holes held the ends of beams. National Park Service photo by A. H. White.

Ruins of a large village called Tyuonyi in Bandelier National Monument.

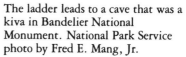

The ladder leads to a cave that was a kiva in Bandelier National Monument. National Park Service photo by Fred E. Mang, Jr.

Prehistoric people, walking from place to place in Bandelier National Monument, wore down trails in the soft rock. National Park Service photo by Natt Dodge.

Ildefonso pueblos along the Rio Grande.

The Museum. A slide program at the museum in the Visitor Center interprets life in the canyon in ancient times. Exhibits show the arts and crafts of the people who lived there.

The Name. The first anthropologist who came west to make a study of sites in New Mexico was Adolph Bandelier. In the late nineteenth century he walked thousands of miles over roadless areas of the state, learning Indian languages, often sleeping on the ground without a blanket, sometimes eating only the parched corn that was a food of the Indians among whom he lived. One of Bandelier's discoveries was the prehistoric settlement in Frijoles Canyon. To explain what he thought life must have been like in this spot he wrote a novel, *The Delight Makers*, which is still very readable and informative. Because of his important services to archeology and his particular connection with Frijoles Canyon, the national monument was named in his honor.

Special Feature. Ninety percent of Bandelier National Monument is a wilderness in which roads will never be built. There are more than 70 miles of trails. Backpacking, with a permit, can be arranged at the visitor center. A recent survey found that there may be as many as 4,000 sites in the monument.

BLACKWATER DRAW,
BLACKWATER DRAW MUSEUM

Midway between Clovis and Portales on US 70. Mail address: ENMU Station 9, Portales, NM 88130. Phone: 505/562-2254. The museum is open Monday—Saturday, afternoon Sunday from Memorial Day to Labor Day; Tuesday—Saturday and afternoon Sunday the rest of the year. The site is open Monday—Saturday, Memorial Day—Labor Day; Saturday and afternoon Sunday from Labor Day—October, and March 1—Memorial Day. Closed November—February. Admission charged: admits visitors to both the museum and the site.

Left:
Petroglyph in a cave, Bandelier National Monument. National Park Service photo by K. Chapman.

Right:
A pictograph at the base of a cliff in Frijoles Canyon, Bandelier National Monument. The Park Service has installed a glass cover to protect it. National Park Service photo by George A. Grant.

This alcove lies at the end of an arduous trail in Bandelier National
Monument. Across the back of the alcove are colored paintings, left there in
prehistoric times. National Park Service photo.

Indians used cooking pits like this in both prehistoric and historic times. Hundreds of these pits are scattered throughout Carlsbad Caverns National Park. National Park Service photo.

This site was discovered by C. W. Anderson and George Roberts, amateur archeologists, at the time when professional archeologists were just realizing that people had been in America for many thousands of years. On the surface, amid old sand dunes, Anderson and Roberts found some distinctive projectile points, together with mammoth bones. Then in August of 1932, Anderson met a professional archeologist, Edgar B. Howard, in Carlsbad, New Mexico. He showed Howard the points and told him about the bones. Howard immediately went to the site. He was much interested in what he saw, and scientific excavation soon began at Blackwater Draw. The distinctive points found there have been called Clovis points after the nearby town.

Hunters who used spear points of the Clovis type roamed widely about 11,000 years ago. Traces of their camps have been found in other parts of the United States as well as at the dig in Blackwater Draw.

Re-examination of a mammoth tusk found in an early excavation here pro-duced evidence that the tusk had been cut off with the same technique used in working ivory in the Upper Paleolithic in Eurasia.

CAPULIN VOLCANO NATIONAL MONUMENT

From Capulin drive 3 miles north on New Mexico 325 to the Visitor Center which is open free, daily, all year. Closed certain holidays. Admission to the monument charged. Mail address: Capulin, NM 88414. Phone: 505/278-2201.

The archeological display in the Visitor Center relates to the Folsom culture. On exhibit are reproductions of Folsom points.

On the road up Capulin Mountain in the monument, there is a distant view of the country around the Folsom site, where artifacts of prehistoric people were first found associated with fossil bones of extinct animals. This site, preserved as Folsom Man State Monument, is unmarked and not accessible to the public.

Archeologists carefully record pictographs in Painted Grotto, in Carlsbad Caverns National Park. National Park Service photo.

CARLSBAD CAVERNS NATIONAL PARK

From Carlsbad drive 18 miles south on US 62, then 7 miles west on park road to the Visitor Center. Mail address: 3225 National Parks Highway, Carlsbad, NM 88220. Phone: 505/785-2232. Open daily, all year except December 25. Admission to the park is free; fees are charged for tours of the caverns. Camping outside park.

Prehistoric Indians apparently never ventured far into Carlsbad Caverns, although they did camp near the cave entrance. They made black and red paintings on the rock wall of the entrance, and they prepared some of their foods in rock-lined cooking pits. Many such pits have been found in the area. Some were constructed later by Apache Indians.

Along the park road in Walnut Canyon visitors may take a self-guided tour, which follows an ethnobotanical trail that identifies plants and the uses to which they were put by Indians of the area. There is also a primitive self-guided trail to Goat Cave.

In the Slaughter Canyon area of the park is Painted Grotto, a pictograph site. Permission to visit this site must be obtained from the superintendent at Park Headquarters.

CASAMERO RUINS

From Grants drive 20 miles west on Interstate 40 to Prewitt exit, then 1 mile east on US 66, then north on county road for about 4.5 miles toward a large electric generating plant. Mail address: Bureau of Land Management, 900 La Plata Highway, Caller Service 4104, Farmington, NM 87499-4104. Phone: 505/325-3581. Open free, at all times.

This site was excavated in the course of salvage archeology conducted at the time the generating plant was being planned. The beautifully made masonry walls and the remains of a great kiva identify it as one of the outlying townships that were connected with Chaco Canyon in the mid-eleventh century (see Chaco Canyon entry). The kiva—about 70 feet in diameter—is one of the largest known. A number of interpretive signs have been put up by the Bureau of Land Management, which administers the ruins.

CHACO CULTURE NATIONAL HISTORICAL PARK
(CHAH-koh)
A World Heritage Site

From US 64 at Bloomfield drive south 28 miles on New Mexico 44, then at Blanco Trading Post take unpaved New Mexico 57, 30 miles to the Visitor Center. Or from Interstate 40 at Thoreau drive north 44 miles on paved New Mexico 57, past Crownpoint, then 20 miles on unpaved New Mexico 57 to the Historical Park. Before leaving Blanco Trading Post or Crownpoint check the condition of the unpaved road ahead. It is sometimes impassable after a rain. Mail address: Star Route 4, Box 6500, Bloomfield, NM 87413. Phone: 505/988-6727 or 6716. Open daily, all year. Admission charged. Camping; water is available but no other supplies.

Here, far from any present-day town, are a dozen large pueblos and over 3,500 smaller sites, the spectacular ruins of a major Anasazi culture center. Easy trails from the main road lead to a number of the most important sites,

and there are self-guided tours at those which have been named Pueblo Bonito, Chetro Ketl, Casa Rinconada and Pueblo Del Arroyo. In the summer, park rangers conduct guided tours through a number of sites, as staffing permits, and there are campfire programs from about Memorial Day to about Labor Day.

Any visit to Chaco Canyon should begin at the Visitor Center, where exhibits in the museum tell the story of human life here. Dioramas and displays help to explain the theories about how people could have prospered in a land that seems dry and desolate.

The Story. The 800 rooms of Pueblo Bonito, a planned, multistory village built in the form of a huge D around a courtyard, were constructed over the course of 300 years. In this pueblo, and in others in the canyon, the art of stonemasonry reached its highest development in the Southwest. Great stretches of wall made from precisely cut and shaped stone remain standing today.

In Chaco Canyon, as elsewhere in the Southwest, a long history of de-

Three examples of the beautiful and distinctive pottery made by the Anasazi people who once inhabited Chaco Canyon. National Park Service photo.

Left:
In the Southwest archeologists find countless potsherds. These broken bits of pottery usually tell who lived at a certain place and even when they lived there. These sherds are all from Chaco Culture National Historical Park. National Park Service photo.

Right:
Stone tools left these marks at the base of a cliff in Chaco Canyon when they were sharpened on a slab of softer sandstone. National Park Service photo by George Grant.

The Great Kiva, Chetro Ketl, Chaco Canyon, after excavation and stabilization. This large ceremonial chamber, once roofed, served a whole community; small kivas were used by local groups. National Park Service photo by George A. Grant.

Different masons worked to build this high building. The walls show four types of stonework, ending with the most painstaking and beautiful in the top story. National Park Service photo by George A. Grant.

After building these walls, masons in Chaco Canyon covered their elegant stonework with a coat of plaster. National Park Service photo.

A wall and door with the ends of three original beams still in place, Chaco Canyon. National Park Service photo by Fred E. Mang, Jr.

velopment lay behind great achievements. It began in the canyon with the Basketmaker people, who by A.D. 400 were building dwellings of the kind called pithouses. They were farmers and craftsmen, quick to adopt new ideas from neighbors or strangers.

Apparently the villages in the canyon were hospitable to outsiders. Groups from other parts of the Southwest may have come in seasonally. By the eleventh century A.D. Chaco had become an important center of activities, the exact nature of which archeologists are still debating. It certainly excelled in producing for trade great quantities of elegant turquoise beads, ornaments and mosaics. Some of the many rooms in the big pueblos may have been for storage of grain, dried meat, and edible wild plant foods. Possibly an exchange system with other communities provided redistribution of all these supplies in times of drought or crop failure.

Traffic to and from the large settlements in the canyon flowed along 300 miles of roads that linked outlying villages with each other and with the center. Some led to distant sources of

supply, even toward Mexico, a source of copper bells, macaws and other exotic things.

Although Chacoans had no burden-carrying animals or wheeled vehicles, they put enormous collective effort into building roads that ran in straight lines uphill and down, across ramps and on stairways where necessary. Many were almost 30 feet wide, excavated in places as deep as 4 or 5 feet to bedrock.

At intervals, adjoining their roads, the Chacoans put up buildings—some large, some small—for what purpose archeologists are not sure. Potsherds have been found scattered along the roads, but no tools used in construction or fires where people might have camped. The function of the roads is still a puzzle. (Elderly Navajos who lived in the area told archeologists that Anasazi people used the "trenches" for protection from giants.)

It was not only goods that Chaco exported over the roads. People from the canyon migrated to other places in the region, taking with them social customs and ceremonial practices and the idea of building preplanned pueblos. About 70 of these outlying town-

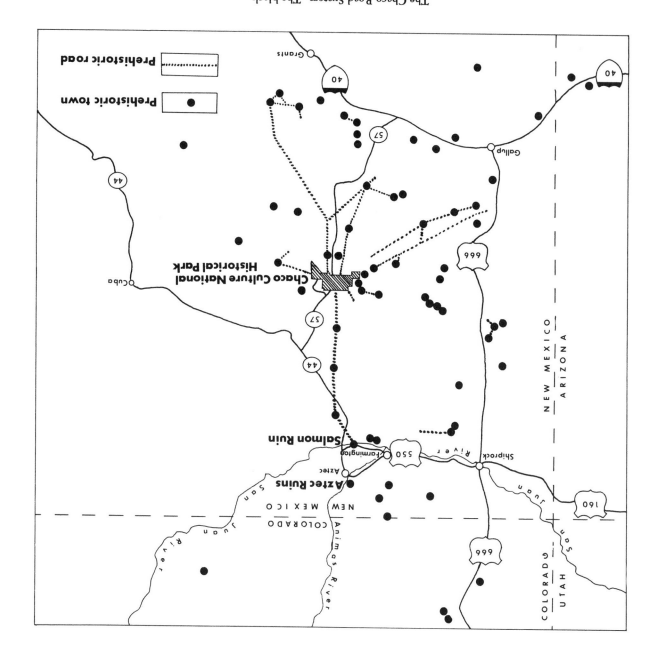

The Chaco Road System. The black
dots indicate the main towns in the
Arizona-Colorado-New Mexico area
that were influenced by the Chaco
culture. Archeologists have
identified nearly 300 miles of
straight roads (dotted lines) linking
some of the towns with each other or
with the great center in Chaco
Canyon.

The dotted lines mark the edges of a 25-foot-wide road, part of the Chacoan communication system. In the background hand-hewn steps carry the road up a slope behind the late Dr. Robert H. Lister, former director of the Chaco Center. National Park Service photo by Thomas H. Wilson.

A group of kivas at Pueblo Bonito seen from the cliff which towers above the site. National Park Service photo by George A. Grant.

Two of the many examples of rock art that appear on cliff faces in Chaco Canyon and many other places in the Southwest. National Park Service photo.

ships have been located and studied. Some archeologists believe that the outliers were settled in order to produce food, which was then transported along the roads to the Chaco center. The settlements consisted of one or more groups of small dwellings and one great kiva, plus a large structure, built in the classic Chaco masonry style, which may have served as a public storehouse for food.

Other archeologists think that the main purpose of the migration to outlying villages was to relieve population pressure at the center. It is generally agreed that at some point the number of people in the canyon grew too large for the agricultural resources of the area. As R. Gwinn Vivian reported to the Society for American Archeology, "Redistribution of population was economically more feasible with primitive transport systems than large-scale redistribution of foodstuffs."

One of these Chacoan outliers may be visited at Salmon Ruins (see entry below), another at Domínguez and Escalante Ruin in Colorado (see entry above), a third at Chimney Rock (see entry above), and still another at Aztec (see entry above).

Besides their architectural and roadbuilding skills, the Chacoans had a talent for constructing irrigation systems and a technical knowledge that enabled them to establish a remarkable astronomical observatory (see above, next page).

In the late part of the twelfth century the greatness of Chaco Canyon came to an end. Archeologists are still debating exactly what pressures led to the abandonment of the canyon. It may well have been that the needs of the people exceeded the resources available, and what Vivian calls "redistribution of population" went on slowly over a number of years. Perhaps the Chacoan phenomenon did not just suddenly and mysteriously collapse. Instead it may have trickled away.

At any rate, the inhabitants of the canyon did eventually depart. After they left, their great buildings filled up gradually with windblown sand and dust, and many of them were only mounds when the first United States soldiers passed through the canyon on an exploring expedition in 1849.

Prehistoric Astronomers

Because it was important for prehistoric people to know when migrations of game would take place or when the time was at hand for planting crops, early hunters and farmers took a keen interest in the sun and moon and stars. Their recurring movements could be correlated with recurring events on earth, and people in widely separated parts of the world developed ways of noting major astronomical events.

In North America modern astronomers and archeologists working together have discovered ancient devices by which it was possible for prehistoric people to know exactly the days of the solstices and equinoxes and other regular occurrences. Sometimes these devices were alignments of stones, as at Bighorn Medicine Wheel in Wyoming. At Cahokia in Illinois circles of posts forming woodhenges were used. In the Southwest some astronomical observations were made by watching where beams of light fell through specially designed windows.

In the Chaco Canyon area of New Mexico ingenious ancient astronomers constructed a sophisticated calendrical device on top of a high butte. In this observatory large slabs of rock were arranged so that shafts of sunlight fell between them onto a group of spiral markings carved into a cliff wall. As the position of the sun changed with the seasons, the shafts of light traversed the face of the markings, indicating important dates to those who knew how to read them.

Skeptical archeologists at first found it hard to believe that accurate observations could be made using three rough-looking stone slabs and some seeming squiggles cut into a cliff. But after careful study they could find no reason to doubt that this was a true astronomical device invented by some Chacoan genius—or geniuses—700 or more years ago.

One geologist made a study of the slabs and concluded that there was no way in which they could have moved accidentally from their original position in the rock of the butte to their present location. In his opinion the slabs must have been moved and positioned by people. Other geologists disagree. They say the ancient Chacoans utilized rocks that had fallen naturally and created from them a marker for the seasons.

The existence and nature of this device, called the Sun Dagger Calendar, was made known to the world by Anna Sofaer, an artist and photographer, who found it while recording the rock art of Chaco Canyon. Whether the slabs were positioned by Chacoans or by nature, Sofaer says, their use indicates remarkable sophistication. Because of recent deterioration, the Park Service has closed Fajada Butte to all visitation.

Archeoastronomy is the name used for the growing new field of study concerned with the astronomical knowledge of prehistoric peoples. This study is making an important contribution to understanding the intellectual achievements of Native Americans.

At the right is a drawing of the shaft of light which has been called the Sun Dagger.

CORONADO STATE MONUMENT

From Albuquerque drive north 20 miles on Interstate 25 to Cuba-Farmington Exit, then 3 miles west on New Mexico 44 to monument entrance. Mail address: P.O. Box 95, Bernalillo, NM 87004. Phone: 505/867-5351. Open Thursday–Monday. Closed certain holidays. Camping.

Here, on the west bank of the Rio Grande River a group of Anasazi people began to make their home about A.D. 1300. By the time the Spanish invaders arrived, in 1540, the pueblo, known as Kuaua (KWAH-wah) had grown tremendously. There were about 1200 ground-level rooms, and above them many other rooms, in places several stories high. The walls of the houses were made of adobe clay, which was moistened and built up in layers, each layer being allowed to dry before the next was added.

In the courtyards of the pueblo were a number of underground ceremonial chambers, or kivas. When archeologists excavated one of them they found murals painted on its plastered walls. Further investigation revealed 17 other layers of plaster underneath, and on each layer were more mural paintings of ceremonial activities. The archeologists worked out an ingenious method of removing the murals a layer at a time. An exhibit in the Visitor Center at the monument tells how they did it. Accurate reproductions of some of the paintings have been put on the wall of a reconstructed kiva at the site.

The people of Kuaua, which means "evergreen" in the Tiwa language, were farmers who grew corn, squash, tobacco, and cotton. They were good weavers and good potters, and they also made fine baskets. Many of their artifacts and religious objects can be seen in the museum at the Visitor Center.

The Name. The monument is named for the leader of the Spanish *conquistadores* who stayed somewhere in the vicinity of Kuaua for a while in the winter of 1540–41.

This is how Pueblo Bonito (in Chaco Canyon) looks when viewed from the top of the cliff. National Park Service photo by George A. Grant.

Pueblo Bonito (Spanish for "beautiful town") is by no means all there is to wonder at in Chaco Canyon, but it was the first to be thoroughly excavated and stabilized. Several other ruins have been explored and studied. Across the arroyo from Pueblo Bonito is Casa Rinconada, where a great kiva has been excavated and sufficiently restored to give an idea of the beauty and majesty of this ceremonial room. Behind the ruin called Kin Kletso an ancient trail leads up through a cleft in the cliff wall to a ruin called Pueblo Alto, on the mesa top.

Many sites in the canyon remain for future archeologists to study, including parts of a possible long-distance, line-of-site signaling network, and there are many aspects of the Chacoan phenomenon still to be understood, even after the completion of an ambitious, ten-year program, in which a number of "space-age" techniques were used.

The treasures of pottery and jewelry that archeologists found here have been removed to museums elsewhere.

Atop the mesa in El Morro National Monument are these ruins of a pueblo built by ancient Zuni Indians. National Park Service photo.

DITTERT SITE

To visit this site, which is south of Grants, make arrangements through the Bureau of Land Management. El Malpais Information Center, 620 E. Santa Fe, Grants, NM 87020. Phone: 505/285-5406.

This site contains about 30 rooms and a kiva. Tree ring dates indicate that the latest construction took place during the thirteenth century. Nearby is a prehistoric roadway and a Great Kiva.

EL MORRO NATIONAL MONUMENT

From Grants drive 43 miles west on New Mexico 53; or from Gallup drive south 30 miles on New Mexico 602, then 24 miles east on New Mexico 53. Mail address: Ramah, NM 87321. Phone: 505/783-4226. Open free, daily, all year. User fee charged for hiking trails. Camping.

Although devoted primarily to preserving inscriptions made in historic times on a 200-foot-high sandstone promontory, this monument includes hundreds of petroglyphs—symbols and designs that Anasazi Indians pecked in the rock long before the first Spaniards arrived. On the mesa behind the cliff stand the ruins of two Pueblo villages, one of which has been partially excavated and stabilized. Visitors may take a self-guided tour of the site, which includes a huge pool that is fed by rains and melted snow, where inhabitants of the pueblos came for water. Handholds and footholds pecked in the rock show the route they followed up and down the cliff.

Exhibits in the Visitor Center interpret the history of the monument, both ancient and modern.

ERNEST THOMPSON SETON MUSEUM
(See Seton Museum)

FLORENCE HAWLEY ELLIS MUSEUM OF ANTHROPOLOGY

At Espanola leave US 285 and fol-low US 84 northwest for 33 miles. At a sign marking "Ghost Ranch Road" (on which is a design of a cow's skull) drive right on a gravel road for 2 miles. *Note:* the museum is *not* at the Ghost Ranch Visitors' Center on US 84. Open free, Tuesday–Saturday; afternoon Sunday. Mail address: Ghost Ranch Conference Center, Abiquiu, NM 87510. Phone: 505/685-4333. Camping.

Exhibits here show the various local peoples and different types of land use from 14,000 B.P. to the end of the nineteenth century. Included are Paleo and Archaic materials and materials from nearby sites of the Gallina cul-ture (eleventh to thirteenth centuries). One exhibit is devoted to Sapawe Pueblo (A.D. 1350–1550), the largest clay-walled pueblo known in New Mexico. According to tradition, the people abandoned Sapawe because of drought and moved to the part of the still-existing San Juan Pueblo that lies on the west bank of the Rio Grande.

FOLSOM MUSEUM

This museum is named in honor of a famous southwestern archeologist who died in 1991.

In the town of Folsom. Mail address: Folsom, NM 88419. Phone: (sum-mer) 505/278-2122; other times: 505/278-2477 or 3616. Open daily, Me-morial weekend–Labor Day weekend; Saturday, Sunday, May and Septem-ber; otherwise by appointment. Ad-mission charged.

This small local history museum in-cludes exhibits related to George McJunkin, the Black cowboy who dis-covered the nearby Folsom Site, which is of great importance to archeology but is not open to the public.

The full story of the discoverer of the Folsom Site is told for young read-ers by one of the authors of this book in *Black Cowboy: The Life and Legend of George McJunkin* which is available at this museum and at the nearby Ca-pulin Volcano National Monument.

Above: A Folsom point. *Right:* Two Clovis points. Clovis points vary in measurement. These (which are pictured here about half actual length) were found along with mammoth bones at the Lehner Site in Arizona. After Haury et al.

Fluted Points

When a projectile point has a channel, or depression, running lengthwise on one or both of its faces, it is said to be fluted. Clovis points, used by mammoth hunters about 11,000 years ago, and Folsom points, used by hunters of very large bison about 10,000 years ago, were fluted.

If fluting had any practical value, it was apparently that the thinned base could easily be inserted into the split end of a spear shaft. However, the labor involved in preparing these points was greater than the labor required to shape an unfluted point. In addition there was a great deal of breakage during manufacture. On the other hand, unfluted points seem to have been equally effective weapons, and they were more durable. This has led some archeologists to suggest that fluting may have had a ceremonial purpose.

How or when or where the practice of fluting began is not known. H. Müller-Beck, a Swiss archeologist, believes it may have started in Europe, possibly in southern Russia, at least 26,000 years ago. Other students of Early Man in America think fluting may have developed on the Bering Land Bridge, where men once hunted mammoths. The Land Bridge is now submerged, so all evidence of what went on there is lost. Still other archeologists believe that fluted points were first made in Alaska or on the southern Great Plains in the United States.

No matter where the custom began, it did not last long, as archeologists measure time. By about 9000 years ago point-makers had shifted from the fragile Folsom points to sturdier points, which were easier to manufacture and less likely to break.

The History of Prehistory

At one time antiquarians were content to say of an object, "This is a projectile point." Then excavators began to name points after the places where they found them. "This is a Clovis point," they said of a point like the ones first found near Clovis, New Mexico. Some museums still go no further with their exhibits.

"What was this point used for?" "What can it tell us about how it was made and about the people who made it?" Archeologists have gone on to try for answers to these questions, too.

"What can this dwelling, or this group of dwellings tell us about the people who made them and about their interaction with their environment? How did this interaction evolve through time?" As they tried to answer such questions archeologists called on men and women from other sciences to help them.

"How can we learn as much as possible and destroy sites as little as possible?" Archeologists had to deal with this question because the number of sites they can study is rapidly dwindling. They want sites and parts of sites to study in the future when they expect to have improved ways of getting information. To do as little damage as possible to evidence of the past, they came to use complex mathematics plus computer analyses and models as they squeezed maximum information from minimal samples.

They have learned how to learn a lot from a little in their race for knowledge against bulldozers making parking lots, against vandals who are interested only in making money from what objects they can sell, and against floods and the ordinary destructiveness of time.

GERONIMO SPRINGS MUSEUM

211 Main Street, Truth or Consequences, NM 87901. Phone: 505/894-6600. Open free, Monday–Saturday. Closed certain holidays.

This museum displays materials from many southwestern cultures including Mimbres, Tularosa, Socorro, Mogollon, Casas Grandes and Anasazi.

GHOST RANCH

(*See Florence Hawley Ellis Museum*)

GHOST RANCH LIVING MUSEUM, GATEWAY TO THE PAST

From Abiquiu drive 15 miles north to sign at entrance. Mail address: Ghost Ranch Living Museum, Abiquiu, NM 87501. Phone: 505/685-4312.

The visitor center and museum here have exhibits on the prehistory of the Chama Gateway Pueblos in the area.

GILA CLIFF DWELLINGS NATIONAL MONUMENT

From Silver City drive 44 miles north on New Mexico 15. Mail address: Rt. 11, Box 100, Silver City, NM 88061. Phone: 505/536-9461. Open free, daily, all year. Closed certain holidays. Camping.

From the trailhead a one-mile roundtrip trail leads along a tree-shaded stream to ruins built in large caves, high above the canyon floor. In summer on Saturday nights, there are evening campfire talks explaining the archeology of the region. Visitors take self-guided tours. Displays in the Visitor Center interpret prehistoric life in the area.

The Story. Perhaps as early as A.D. 100, Mogollon people began to live within the borders of the present monument. They grew corn and beans, and for about 900 years they built dwellings that archeologists call pithouses because the floor was below ground level. About A.D. 1000, new ideas began to filter in from the Pueblo Indians

Above and opposite: Some of the houses built in alcoves at Gila Cliff Dwellings National Monument. National Park Service photo by Parker Hamilton.

to the north. Square stone houses above ground took the place of pithouses. New kinds of white pottery, decorated with black designs, were also borrowed from the north, replacing the older red-on-brown ware.

The Mogollon built some of the new, square-roomed dwellings in caves in the cliffs, and some of these are the structures that have been stabilized and prepared for visitors to the monument.

About A.D. 1300 the houses were all abandoned. No one knows why the inhabitants left or where they went. After they moved away, Apache Indians settled in the area, but they did not become cliff dwellers.

GRAN QUIVIRA
(gran kee-VEE-rah)
(Unit of Salinas Pueblo Missions National Monument)

From Mountainair on US 60 drive south 26 miles on New Mexico 55. Mail address: P.O. Box 498, Mountainair, NM 87036. Phone: 505/847-2770. Open free, daily. Closed December 25 and January 1.

Adjacent to the ruined Spanish mission at Gran Quivira is Las Humanas, largest of the Salinas pueblos. Las Humanas was an important trading center before and after the Spanish occupation.

The Story. People built pithouses of the Mogollon type in this area about A.D. 800. About A.D. 1100 they began to get ideas from the Anasazi who lived to the west. Soon black-on-white pottery became popular, and much the same lifeway came to be observed here as in the pueblos in the Rio Grande Valley. There was also trade with the Plains Indians.

One mound at the site contains more than 200 rooms built between A.D. 1300 and A.D. 1600. The remains of burned and filled kivas here mark the efforts of Spanish priests to abolish native religion. But the pueblo religious leaders simply turned an above-ground room into a ceremonial chamber in which to continue their traditional rituals.

The Museum. In the Visitor Center are display cases showing artifacts in their relation to the development of the culture of the people who lived here. An award-winning, forty-minute film of the excavation of one of the 21 house mounds at the site will be shown on request. A ten-minute video is also available. A self-guided tour leads through the site.

GUADALUPE RUIN

To visit this site, which is in a remote area northeast of Grants and cannot be reached in wet weather, contact: Bureau of Land Management, Rio Puerco Resource Area, 435 Montano Road NE, Albuquerque, NM 87107. Phone: 505/761-4504.

Here a 25 room pueblo with three kivas sits atop a sheer-sided butte above the Rio Puerco. It was built in the mid-900s, abandoned about A.D. 1130, then reoccupied and remodeled extensively during the thirteenth century.

HAWIKUH
(See Zuni below)

Excavators at work at Gran Quivira, a unit of Salinas Pueblo Missions National Monument, where ruins of both Spanish and prehistoric Indian structures have been preserved. National Park Service photo by Fred E. Mang, Jr.

Ike Lovato, one of the Jemez Indian rangers who interpret Giusewa, which was built by their ancestors.

Ruins at Jemez State Monument. Museum of New Mexico photo.

HUPOBI RUIN

To make arrangements to see this site contact Bureau of Land Management, Taos Resource Area, Plaza Montevideo Building, Cruz Alta Road, P.O. Box 6168, Taos, NM 87571-6168. Phone: 505/758-8851.

This 1,000 room Anasazi adobe pueblo was occupied between A.D. 1300 and 1500. At the site are petroglyphs and extensive grid gardens.

JEMEZ STATE MONUMENT (HEM-ess)

From Bernalillo drive 23 miles northwest on New Mexico 44, then northeast on New Mexico 4 to monument entrance on the northern edge of the town of Jemez Springs. Or from Los Alamos drive 38 miles west and south on New Mexico 4. Mail address: P.O. Box 143, Jemez Springs, NM 87025. Phone: 505/829-3530. Open daily. Closed certain holidays. Admission charged.

Here are the ruins of the pueblo of Giusewa (jee-SAY-wah), which dates from about A.D. 1300. It is known to have been very large, but how large is uncertain, because only part of it has been excavated. In places the buildings are three stories high.

The prehistoric inhabitants used the nearby hot springs as baths. Today their descendants live several miles down the canyon, in Jemez Pueblo. They are the only people who now speak the Towa language.

Rangers at the monument are members of Jemez Pueblo, and they have participated in preparing the museum exhibits at the Visitor Center. Displays interpret the life and history of Giusewa from the Indian point of view, with an audio accompaniment of traditional Jemez music. There are additional interpretive panels along the trail through the ruins.

The monument, a unit of the Museum of New Mexico, also preserves the seventeenth-century Franciscan mission of San José de los Jemez.

MAXWELL MUSEUM OF ANTHROPOLOGY

(See University of New Mexico)

MILLICENT ROGERS MUSEUM

From Taos drive 4 miles north to directional sign near the junction of US 64 and New Mexico 3. Phone: 505/758-2462. Open daily, all year. Admission charged.

In addition to modern Native American material, this museum exhibits some fine Mimbres and Anasazi pottery.

MUSEUM OF INDIAN ARTS AND CULTURE

710 Camino Lejo, Santa Fe, NM 87501. Phone: 505/827-8941. Open daily. Admission charged.

In addition to contemporary arts and crafts, exhibits here are taken from the extensive collections of prehistoric artifacts held by the Laboratory of Anthropology which is open only to scholars and researchers. Scheduled for

KIT CARSON HISTORIC MUSEUM

On Old Kit Carson Rd., one-half block east of the plaza, Taos (TOWSS). Mail address: P.O. Drawer CCC, Taos, NM 87571. Phone: 505/758-0505. Open daily, all year. Closed certain holidays. Admission charged.

One room in this museum is devoted to Native American culture and includes exhibits of prehistoric material from the Taos area dating back as far as 3000 B.C. Most of the archeological material is Anasazi from after the year A.D. 1.

LOS ALAMOS HISTORICAL MUSEUM

On Central Avenue near 20th Street. Mail address: P.O. Box 43, Los Alamos, NM 87544. Phone: 505/662-6272. Open free, Monday–Saturday, afternoon Sunday. Closed certain holidays.

In the first room, in addition to displays about the geology of the area, are exhibits of artifacts that illuminate the lives of the hunters and farmers who lived on the Pajarito Plateau from A.D. 100 to 1500.

The Palace of the Governors, Santa Fe, is the oldest governmental building on the soil of the United States. Spanish colonial authorities established it about A.D. 1609. In the arcade along the front of the building Indians from various pueblos sell their craftwork. Inside is a small archeological exhibit. Photo by Russell D. Butcher.

Virginia Pecos once served as a Ranger at the home of her ancestors in Pecos National Historic Park. National Park Service photo by Fred E. Mang, Jr.

the next few years are changing exhibits of prehistoric jewelry, stone work and Mimbres archeology.

NEW MEXICO STATE UNIVERSITY MUSEUM

On the campus of New Mexico State University, on University Ave., off US 80, Interstate 25, and Interstate 10, Las Cruces. Mail address: Box 3564, Las Cruces, NM 88003. Phone: 505/646-3739. Open free. Tuesday–Saturday, afternoon Sunday.

This general museum contains Mogollon pottery and stone tools from the period A.D. 800 to 1350, together with a considerable quantity of Casas Grandes pottery from northern Mexico. Exhibits also include local archeological finds and much ethnological material.

PALACE OF THE GOVERNORS

Palace Ave., on the Plaza, Santa Fe. Open free, daily, Tuesday–Sunday, mid-October–mid-March. Closed certain holidays. Administered by the Museum of New Mexico, P.O. Box 2087, Santa Fe, NM 87504. Phone: 505/827-6344.

This handsome building was formerly the governor's residence under Spanish colonial, territorial and recent administrations. Erected in 1609, it has been in use continuously since then.

At one time the exhibits here included much prehistoric as well as historic material. Now only one room, the Nusbaum Room, recreates the museum's first archeological exhibit of material from the Pajarito Plateau. The Museum of Indian Arts and Culture (see above) has taken responsibility for displaying archeological material.

PECOS NATIONAL HISTORICAL PARK
(PAY-kohs)

From Santa Fe drive southeast 25 miles on Interstate 25 to Glorieta-Pecos exit, then 6 miles on State Road 50, turn right on State Road 63, 2 miles to the park. Or from Las Vegas drive west on Interstate 25 to Rowe exit, then 5 miles on State Road 63 to the park. Mail address: P.O. Drawer 418, Pecos, NM 87552-0418. Phone: 505/757-6414. Open daily, all year. Closed certain holidays. Admission charged. Camping nearby.

Here, near the Pecos River, are the ruins of a pueblo that housed one of the largest town populations north of Mexico, when Coronado entered the area in 1541. Visitors may follow a trail on a self-guided tour of the ruins.

The Story. In the ninth century people began to settle in small groups along the upper reaches of the river. In time these small settlements grew together into larger settlements, and by 1540 Pecos was a huge, multistoried pueblo, constructed around an open plaza. At least 660 rooms provided living quarters for about 2,000 people.

The Pecos people were farmers, like the Anasazi, but their geographic location led them into special activities. Their pueblo stood at a crossroads, where Plains Indians met Pueblo Indians from the Rio Grande Valley, and where Indians from north and south along the Pecos River met. The pueblo center which also has a 12-minute introductory film on Pecos history.

Dr. Kidder's discoveries made it possible to bring order into the chronology of a large area in the Southwest. In 1927 all archeologists who had been working in the area came to Pecos to exchange information and to adopt a terminology that all of them could use and understand. Honoring that first Southwestern conference, archeologists still meet every year for a Pecos Conference at some place in the Southwest.

PETROGLYPH NATIONAL MONUMENT

In Albuquerque, on Atrisco Drive NW, about one-half mile north of Taylor Ranch. Mail address: P.O. Box 1293, Albuquerque, NM 87103. Phone: 505/873-6620. Open daily. Admission charged.

From about A.D. 1300 to 1680 prehistoric Puebloan Indians carved a variety of realistic and symbolic drawings in the face of the basaltic escarpment created by a lava flow from a nearby

was a great center for trade. Many strangers came there.

Sometime in the 1620s a Franciscan priest built a huge church near Pecos and set about Christianizing the inhabitants. Apparently his success was incomplete. The pueblo continued to use ceremonial kivas.

In 1680 the Pecos people joined most of the other Pueblo Indians in a general revolt against the Spanish. They burned the church and drove the friars out. The church building which stands at Pecos today is much smaller than the original mission, signs of which were discovered only in 1967, during archeological excavations.

By 1838 the population of Pecos had dwindled from 2,000 to 17. Disease had killed many. Warfare killed others. The survivors moved to Jemez Pueblo, where their descendants live today.

Between 1915 and 1929 Dr. A. V. Kidder made very important excavations at the Pecos site. A vast number of interesting artifacts came from the dig. This collection is at Pecos and part of it is exhibited at the visitor

Pecos Indians built this wall not for defense but to outline the area of the town which was closed to visitors at night. National Park Service photo.

Pecos ruins, which were first investigated by Adolph Bandelier, who drove out in a buggy from Santa Fe, 25 miles away. National Park Service photo.

Grizzlier than Grizzlies

At the time when Paleo-Indians were hunting huge ice-age mammals 10,900 years ago, a giant short-faced bear went into a cave in what is now New Mexico. A hundred feet into the cave, in pitch blackness, the animal fell down a rock chimney. As it struggled to climb back out, it left claw marks on the cave wall. Probing around in the dark, it wandered farther and fell down another chimney, this time to its death.

In 1976 cave explorers found the animal's skeleton which was later identified as a bear that was bigger and faster and hence more dangerous than a Kodiak grizzly. That was one of the creatures with which the First Americans shared North America.

---

volcano. Several concentrated groups of petroglyphs are protected and interpreted within the monument, and self-guided tours to them may be taken along prepared trails. The National Park Service offers guided tours to other areas of the monument.

PICURIS PUEBLO
(pee-koo-REES)

From Taos drive southwest on New Mexico 68 to Embudo, then east about 16 miles on New Mexico 75. Mail address: P.O. Box 127, Penasco, NM 87553.

Archeological excavations at Picuris have established that the pueblo was founded between A.D. 1250 and 1300. Those who built their homes at the present site moved from another pueblo that once stood near Talpa (on New Mexico 3). The excavated features at Picuris are open to the public and may be photographed.

POSHU OINGE
(PO-shoe WIN-gay)

On US 84 about 2 miles east of Abiquiu. Mail address: Santa Fe National Forest, 1220 St. Francis Drive, Santa Fe, NM 87504. Phone: 505/988-6940. Open free, at all times.

Here are the remains of a pueblo from the fourteenth and fifteenth centuries that has about 500 rooms. A trail with interpretive signs leads to it.

Ancestors of the present-day inhabitants of Santa Clara Pueblo once lived in these rooms at Puyé Ruins. Photo by Ellen Conried Balch.

Reproduction of a painting of the Squash Blossom Girl, part of a mural found in a kiva in Awatovi, an ancient village on the Hopi Reservation.

A general view of Puyé Cliff, showing some of the masonry structures at the base together with holes leading into artificial caves in the cliff itself. Photo by Ellen Conried Balch.

Ruins of the old Quarai mission stand amid remains of a prehistoric pueblo in Salinas Pueblo Missions National Monument. Museum of New Mexico photo.

PUYÉ CLIFF RUINS, SANTA CLARA INDIAN RESERVATION
(poo-YAY)

From Espanola on US 84 drive southwest on New Mexico 30 to directional sign, then 9 miles west on New Mexico 5 to entrance gate. Mail address: Tourism Dept., Santa Clara Pueblo, P.O. Box 580, Espanola, NM 87532. Phone: 505/753-7326. Open all year. Admission charged. Camping nearby.

Ancestors of the present-day Santa Clara Indians lived at Puyé Cliff. Some of their masonry dwellings were built along the base of the rock wall, other rooms were dug into the soft stone of the cliff itself, and on top of the cliff were several hundred additional rooms. Apparently the inhabitants moved away from Puyé Cliff seeking more fertile and better-watered lands, which they found near the site of the present Santa Clara Pueblo.

Parts of this very large ruin have been excavated and prepared for view by the public. The site is one of the few large prehistoric ruins administered by the descendants of the people who once lived there.

QUARAI
(car-EYE)
(Unit of Salinas Pueblo Missions National Monument)

From Mountainair on US 60 drive north on New Mexico 55, 8 miles to Punta de Agua, then 1 mile west from directional sign. Open free. Closed certain holidays. Camping nearby.

In addition to walls of a seventeenth-century Spanish mission that can be seen here, there are many unexcavated pueblo ruins. Archeological tests show that one part of the site was inhabited in the fourteenth and fifteenth centuries. Historical documents record that these people spoke the Tiwa language.

Before the Indians and Spaniards abandoned Quarai in the 1670s, it served occasionally as the center for the Inquisition in New Mexico. Although the Indians, considered inferiors, were not subject to the Inquisition, they still had to pay tithes to the state and did not escape punishment if they practiced ancient rituals.

The museum at Quarai has displays of prehistoric and historic artifacts that interpret life at Quarai. A self-guided trail leads .33 miles past unexcavated ruins and through the mission.

SALINAS PUEBLO MISSIONS NATIONAL MONUMENT
(sah-LEE-nus)

This monument consists of three separate units, located in three places: Abó (see above) and Quarai (see above), which were formerly New Mexico State Monuments, and Gran Quivira (see above), which was formerly a National Monument by itself. All three units were unified in 1981 to form the current Salinas Pueblo Missions National Monument. The Headquarters for the monument is located one block west of the intersection of US 60 and New Mexico 55 in Mountainair, New Mexico. Here, an informational audio-visual program introduces the visitor to the monument. Open free, daily, except certain holidays. For information write to: Salinas Pueblo Missions National Monument, P.O. Box 496, Mountainair, NM 87036. Phone: 505/847-2585.

RED ROCK STATE PARK MUSEUM

Five miles east of Gallup, just north of US 66. Mail address: P.O. Box 328, Church Rock, NM 87311. Phone: 505/863-1337. Open free, daily, Memorial Day–Labor Day. Remainder of the year, Monday–Friday. Permanent, revolving, and temporary exhibits interpret the past and present Native American cultures of the Four Corners Region. The museum includes archeological displays. *Special Interest.* The park is the home of the Inter-Tribal Indian Ceremonial held in August each year as well as Indian dances every evening during the summer months.

SALMON RUIN
(SOL-mun)

From Bloomfield drive 2.5 miles west on US 64 to entrance and museum. Mail address: P.O. Box 125, Bloomfield, NM 87413. Phone: 505/632-2013. Open daily, all year. Closed certain holidays. Admission charged. Camping nearby.

The Salmon pueblo was one of several built by people who were influ-

Archeologists excavating Salmon Ruin. Photo by Peter B. George.

Part of the museum at Salmon Ruin, which was financed by a bond issue approved by citizens of San Juan County.

Fanciful Archeology

The Swiss writer Erich von Daniken has started a fad that attracts people who are more interested in believing than in knowing. Without any evidence, often citing data inaccurately, and with disrespect for the abilities of Native Americans, he claims that many archeological features in the Americas were created by visitors from outer space. Although a carefully researched television program demonstrated to millions of viewers that there is no basis in fact for von Daniken's theories, believers persist.

Other theories, too, have been based on the racist notion that Indians had to get their ideas from somewhere else. At one time or another the Celts, the Welsh, the Irish, Phoenicians, Egyptians, and Africans were all put forward as originators of great achievements in the New World. The American Indians themselves were supposed by some to have been descended from the Ten Lost Tribes of Israel.

That fancies flourish where facts are few
Is true of Atlantis and also of Mu.

A tourist rests at the entrance to Sandia Cave, after climbing the spiral stairway from the path, far below.

---

enced by developments in the Chaco Canyon area, about 50 miles to the south. Tree-ring dates taken from roof beams show that the massive masonry structures were put up between A.D. 1088 and 1095. Built in the form of a squared C, the pueblo measured 430 feet along the back wall, 150 feet along the arms and was two stories high. In this preplanned, multiple dwelling were about 250 large, high-ceilinged rooms, arranged in groups for family units. Underground in the plaza was a ceremonial Great Kiva and, at the highest point in the structure, an unusual tower kiva.

After about 60 years of occupation, most of the first settlers left the pueblo. Only a few of the original inhabitants remained; then in the thirteenth century new people moved in, probably from the San Juan River valley. They made pottery in the style of Mesa Verde, and their culture seems to have been simpler than that of the Chacoans. They divided the large, orignal rooms into smaller units, by constructing poorly made masonry walls. By the beginning of the fourteenth century, these people, too, had abandoned the pueblo.

The ruin has been partially excavated and is undergoing stabilization. It can be visited on a self-guided tour. The San Juan County Archaeological Research Center and Museum at the site has exhibits of materials found there. The museum is the result of a cooperative endeavor by the citizens of San Juan County, who voted a $275,000 bond issue to finance construction of the Research Center and Library.

Excavation and interpretation of this important site were directed by the late Dr. Cynthia Irwin-Williams.

The Name. Salmon Ruin was named for George Salmon, who homesteaded in the area in the late 1800s and protected the site from vandals and pothunters.

Special Interest. In Heritage Park at the Salmon Ruin, reconstructions interpret Native American life of the past 10,000 years. Here are examples of many different artifacts and types of dwelling.

SANDIA CAVE
(san-DEE-ah)

Administered by the Forest Service of the U.S. Department of Agriculture. Mail address: 2113 Osuna Rd., Suite A, Albuquerque, NM 87113. Phone: 505/762-4650.

This cave is of interest because for many years archeologists believed that it had contained the oldest artifacts found in America. The remains of human occupation were originally dated at about 20,000 years B.P. (before present). Re-study of the material has cast doubt on this early date, but the cave does remain of interest as one of the two places in which Sandia points have been found. These points seem to be at least as old as the Clovis points that have been associated with the hunting of mammoths.

Material from the excavation is in the Museum of Anthropology, University of New Mexico, Albuquerque.

Prehistoric Firepower

Stone weapons changed a great deal in the millennia of their use. Very early in the Old World people learned to extend their grasp by jabbing a pointed stick into small creatures they could not easily reach with their bare hands. They also learned how to break certain kinds of stone to get sharp edges that were good for cutting or gouging. Then came a big innovation. Someone fastened a stick and a sharpened rock together— and made a spear.

At first this new tool was probably used only for poking, but it was effective. In America humans could apparently kill even mammoths with thrusting spears. They increased the range of their weapons when they found they could hurl a spear as well as thrust it. The spear had become a javelin—a projectile. Next its range was extended with the aid of a spear-thrower, also called a throwing stick or atlatl (AT-ul-AT-ul). People who used atlatls often made the shafts of their spears lighter than the shafts of thrusting spears, and these small spears, or javelins, are often called darts. Dart points, too, were likely to be smaller than the points on heavy thrusting spears.

For thousands of years American Indians got much of their protein food with the aid of darts and atlatls. Then came a device with which a person could put still more power behind projectiles—the bow. The bow acted as a spring; it stored up muscle power and then released a lot of it all at once.

As people increased the power behind the projectile, they were often able to decrease the size of the projectile shaft. For the sake of balance, the lighter shaft was equipped with a light point. Even reeds were used as the forepart of dart shafts and also for arrows, and some arrow points were very small.

Since arrows were easily transported in quantity, they made possible a great increase in firepower, and human destructiveness multiplied. Not only could they kill more animals and thus obtain more food; they could also kill more people. So, paradoxically, as soon as human beings were better able to provide for themselves, they also became less sure of surviving.

Archeologists may never know how it happened that some genius invented the bow. They do know that it appeared in the Old World and then in the New. Exactly how it got to the New World is not clear. Some archeologists speculate that it may have been re-invented here. It was in the Arctic about 4000 years ago. Its spread southward seems to have been slow. Apparently Southwestern people did not hunt with the bow and arrow until shortly after A.D. 200. The Plains people did not use the bow and arrow until even later.

The wood that went into making bows varied from place to place, depending on what was available. Some were made of several small pieces of wood ingeniously fitted together. Some were reinforced with sinews. Bows were long. Bows were short. Bows curved in different ways. Some arrows may have been only sharpened wooden sticks. Some shafts were made of sturdy reeds. Very often a man identified his own arrows by painting some special mark or symbol on them.

Arrow points are abundant in areas where people depended heavily on hunting for food. In other areas, where most of the food came from agriculture, arrow points may be much less frequently found. In the largest ruins of the Southwest, for example, they are often far from numerous.

The spear-thrower, also called a throwing-stick or atlatl, extended the distance a spear could travel and the force with which it could be hurled. After Indians discovered the greater accuracy and efficiency of the bow and arrow, they generally stopped using the atlatl and dart. Atlatls were still in use, however, when De Soto encountered Native Americans on the Louisiana coast in 1543.

Taos Pueblo as it appears today.

SAN JUAN PUEBLO
(san-HWAN)

About 5 miles north of Española on New Mexico 68 and US 285. Mail address: Española, NM 87532. Phone: 505/852-4400. Open free, daylight hours. A visitor's permit must be obtained from the governor of the pueblo. Camping nearby.

This pueblo was in existence when the first Spaniards arrived. The name San Juan is a shortened form of San Juan de los Caballeros, the name given the pueblo by the Spanish conquerors.

SANTA CLARA PUEBLO

From Santa Fe drive north 30 miles on US 84-285 to Española; cross the Rio Grande and turn south on New Mexico 5, 2 miles to the pueblo. Mail address: P.O. Box 580, Española, NM 87532. Phone: 505/753-7326. Open free, daily, all year. Camping nearby.

This pueblo has apparently been on its present site about 800 years. Santa Clarans call themselves "Kha'p'ong" or "The People of the Singing Water." In earlier prehistoric times the Santa Clara people lived on the Pajarito Plateau, in the region of Puyé.

SETON MUSEUM

From Cimarron drive 5 miles south on New Mexico 21 to Philmont Camping Headquarters. Mail address: Philmont Scout Ranch, Cimarron, NM 87714. Open free, June 1–August 31, and Monday–Friday, September 1–May 31.

From its large collections of archeological and ethnological artifacts the museum offers exhibits that depict the life and culture of the Southwest.

TAOS PUEBLO
(TOWSS)

From Taos drive north 3 miles on New Mexico 3. Mail address: Taos, NM 87571. Phone: 505/758-4604. Open daily, all year. Parking fee required. Visitors may take photographs on payment of a fee. Camping nearby.

This pueblo has existed on its present site since prehistoric times, and the architecture of the buildings resembles the architecture of the pre-Spanish pueblo.

VILLAGE VISTA SITE

About 15 miles northeast of Mimbres. Mail address: Forest Service, Mimbres Ranger District, P.O. Box 79, Mimbres, NM 88049. Phone: 505/536-2250. Open free, all year. As this book went to press, the site was being prepared for handicapped access.

Here is a site, with interpretive signs, once occupied by people of the Mimbres culture.

WESTERN NEW MEXICO UNIVERSITY MUSEUM

On the campus at 10th St. in Silver City. Mail address: P.O. Box 680, Silver City, NM 88062. Phone: 505/538-6386. Open Monday–Friday, afternoon. Closed Saturday and Sunday. Closed school holidays.

Here is the largest display of Mimbres pottery in the world. Its unique, idiosyncratic designs are often copied in commercial pottery. Also on display are some Casas Grandes and other prehistoric material.

ZIA PUEBLO (TSEE-ah)

From Bernalillo drive northwest 18 miles on NM 44. Open free, during daylight hours. Visitors are not allowed to photograph, draw, or paint in the pueblo. Camping nearby.

This pueblo has been on its present site since about A.D. 1300. Excavations by the late Dr. Cynthia Irwin-Williams suggest that the ancestors of the Zia people, like the ancestors of some other Pueblo people, have lived in the same general area for nearly 8000 years.

The symbol for the sun that the ancient Zia used has been adopted as the design at the center of the New Mexico state flag. These are the words of the official salute to the flag: "I salute the Zia symbol of perfect friendship among united cultures."

THREE RIVERS PETROGLYPH NATIONAL RECREATION SITE

Drive 28 miles south from Carrizozo (care-ee-SO-so) on US 54, then 5 miles east at Three Rivers, following signs on a gravel road. Phone: 505/525-8828. Open free, all year. Camping nearby.

A 1400-yard surfaced trail, with shaded rests along the way, leads through an area where people of the Jornada branch of the Mogollon culture made more than 500 rock carvings between the years A.D. 900 and 1400. Pictured on the jumbled boulders here are ceremonial figures, geometric figures, and animals—birds, frogs, lizards, mountain sheep, insects, and even an inchworm. Especially interesting are large, decorative pictures of fish in this very arid part of the country. Found here and almost nowhere else is a recurring design, made of a circle surrounded by dots.

TWIN ANGELS PUEBLO

Access to this site requires a four-wheel drive vehicle and a strenuous hike. Arrangements to visit should be made through the Bureau of Land Management, Farmington Resource Area, 1235 La Plata Highway, Farmington, NM 87401. Phone: 505/327-5344.

This 20-room pueblo with two kivas is perched on a sheer cliff overlooking Kutz Canyon. It was built between A.D. 1050 and 1150.

UNIVERSITY OF NEW MEXICO, MAXWELL MUSEUM OF ANTHROPOLOGY

On the campus, at University and Ash, N.E., Albuquerque 87131. Phone: 505/277-4404. Open free, Monday–Saturday, afternoon Sunday. Closed certain holidays.

This excellent museum emphasizes archeology of the Southwest and in addition contains exhibits of archeological and ethnological material from other parts of the world. Permanent exhibits include *People of the Southwest* and *Ancestors*. Rotating exhibits feature various subjects, including archeological material from the Gilbert and Dorothy Maxwell Collection.

ZUNI PUEBLO
(ZOON-yee or ZOON-ee)

From Gallup drive south 30 miles on New Mexico 602, then 11 miles west on New Mexico 53. Open free, at any time. Arrangements for photographing must be made through the Zuni Tribal Office, Zuni, NM 87327, or phone: 505/782-2525. Camping nearby.

Zuni Indians have lived on or near the site of the present town since prehistoric times. About 50 miles south of the pueblo is the sacred Zuni Salt Lake, in the crater of an extinct volcano. Since ancient times the Zuni and other Indians have gathered salt there.

Other places of archeological interest on the Zuni Reservation are:

A:shiwi A:wan Museum and Heritage Center

In Zuni on the south side of State Highway 53. Mail address: Zuni Museum Project, P.O. Box 339, Zuni, NM 87237. Phone: 505/782-5559.

The mission of this new museum is to facilitate the interpretation of Zuni history and culture, to serve as a culture resource center for the Zuni community and to enhance cross-cultural awareness. Small exhibits are on display.

Hawikuh
(hah-wee-KOO)

About 12 miles south of Zuni Pueblo, Zuni Indian Reservation. For permission to visit the site, for the services of a guide, and information about fee, apply to Zuni Tribal office (see Village of the Great Kivas below).

Archeologists investigated this site in the early twentieth century, but did not do anything to stabilize the ruins they found here. As a result there remain for the most part only mounds of rubble, covered with potsherds and debris. However, a visit may be worthwhile in view of the history of the place.

The Story. Hawikuh was a town of perhaps 1500 people when Spanish explorers entered the Southwest in 1539, led by a Franciscan monk, Friar Marcos. With him came the famous Black slave, Estevan, who had accompanied Cabeza de Vaca on a seemingly impossible journey from the Gulf Coast north through Texas, then south to Mexico City.

While Marcos and Estevan were still in Mexico, they heard from Indians that there were seven fabulously rich cities of Cibola to the north. Marcos sent Estevan on ahead of his expedition, and at Hawikuh the Black explorer met his death.

Estevan had traveled far, had visited many people who lived as hunters and gatherers, and was skilled at getting along with them. A persuasive explanation of his death at Hawikuh seems to be that he arrived there in the company of wandering Indians who had joined Marcos and who belonged to groups that had given the sedentary Zunis a great deal of trouble. More important, Estevan looked different from any people the Zunis had ever seen—black skin, curly hair and beard—and he was dressed as if he might be a shaman or medicine man. The priests at Hawikuh, who were not shamans, were taking no chances with potential rivals in the field of religion, and Estevan's large following gave the impression that he might be regarded as having special powers. So the first Black explorer in North America, who happened also to be the first explorer from the Old World to enter New Mexico from Old Mexico, was killed by Zuni arrows.

Meanwhile Friar Marcos returned to Mexico City with tales of the Seven Cities of Cibola, one of which—Hawikuh—he claimed he had seen, although he had not been near the place. It was this hoax that sparked Coronado's expedition through the Southwest and changed the history of the people who lived there.

Village of the Great Kivas

On the Zuni Indian Reservation. For road directions and permission to visit the site, write: Zuni Tribal Office, Zuni, NM 87327, or phone: 505/782-2525.

This small, ruined settlement is notable for the two Great Kivas which identify it as one of the outliers, or colonies, established by people from Chaco Canyon (see entry above) in the eleventh century.

Tree-Ring Dating

Trees grow by adding layers of wood outside the layers that are already there. Some trees add a layer each year, and in years that are wet during the growing season, the layers are thick. In dry years they are thin. In an area where weather conditions are uniform, all trees that are weather-sensitive in this way tend to have the same pattern of thick and thin rings. By matching the ring pattern in a living tree with the ring pattern in a tree that was felled some time ago, it is often possible to tell the exact year in which the dead tree was cut.

Working backward from living trees, scientists have found a pattern of tree-ring growth that prevailed in much of the Southwest for many hundreds of years. They have made a master chart showing patterns of clusters of thick rings and thin rings. These patterns are called signatures, and each tree-ring signature differs from every other just as each handwritten signature differs from every other. By comparing the pattern of growth rings in a tree with the master chart it is possible to determine the exact years during which the tree was alive. In this way you can find out the exact year when the tree died or was cut down.

If the tree was used as a beam in a room, you can be sure it was not used before it was cut down. You have the beginning of a date for the room. If you find other beams in the same room all with the same date, you can be fairly sure when the roof was put on the building. If you find charcoal in the fireplace of the building that gives the same date as the roof beams, you can be reasonably sure that the building was finished and used in about the year given by the tree rings in the beams. This also means that you have some idea about the date of artifacts found in the room. The entire contents of the room were not likely to have been placed there before the room was built.

Tree-ring dating is also called dendrochronology.

Cross section showing growth rings

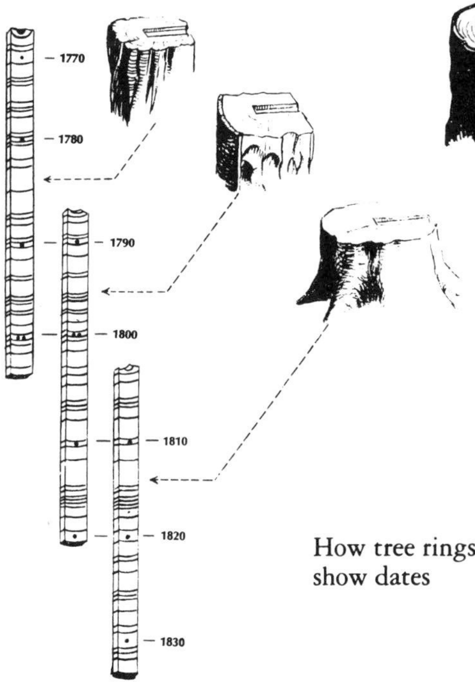

How tree rings can show dates

Drawing by Ursula Koering

Are they dancers? These petroglyphs are near a site called Sand Island west of Bluff, Utah. Photo by Julia M. Johnson; copyright by Julia M. Johnson.

Utah

ALKALI RIDGE

From Monticello drive 13 miles south on US 191 to directional marker, then 8 miles to site. Or from Blanding drive 5 miles north on US 191 to directional marker, then 2 miles to site. Open free, at all times. Camping nearby.

Although no exhibits have been prepared for the public here, the site has long been of interest to archeologists. More than a thousand years ago a band of people settled in this land of cliffs and canyons. They hunted bighorn sheep, planted small fields of corn, and found it a good place in which to live. Their descendants continued to make their homes there for 500 years.

The firstcomers belonged to an early group of Anasazi people, called Basketmakers because they were very skilled at weaving baskets of many kinds. As time passed they developed new skills, following the general pattern of all the Anasazi in the region. Students of archeology are especially interested in this settlement at Alkali Ridge, because they can trace Anasazi life there, stage by stage, and also because the ceremonial kivas, which mark Anasazi culture in the Southwest, may have evolved in this particular area.

Alkali Ridge was excavated between 1931 and 1933 by J. O. Brew, of the Peabody Museum, at Harvard. Afterward, the site itself was covered over, and there is little for the casual visitor to see.

ANASAZI INDIAN VILLAGE STATE PARK

In Boulder on Utah 12. Mail address: P.O. Box 1329, Boulder, UT 84716. Phone: 801/335-7308. Open daily, all year. Admission charged. Camping nearby.

About 200 people occupied this village, also called the Coombs Site, from about A.D. 1050 to 1200. A self-guided tour leads through the site in which nearly 90 rooms have been excavated. A reconstructed six-room dwelling shows how the Anasazi lived. In the museum are a diorama of the original village, artifacts recovered from the site and exhibits relating to Anasazi culture.

ARCH CANYON RUIN

From Blanding drive south on US 191 to intersection with Utah 95, then about 20 miles west to the bottom of Comb Wash marked by a small sign, then north 3 miles on a graded road which ends at the head of a trail leading $^{1}/_{4}$ mile to the site. Open free, at all times. Camping nearby.

This small ineresting Anasazi ruin has been partially stabilized and fenced to keep out cattle, but can be entered through a gate. For more information inquire at Bureau of Land Management, P.O. Box 7, Monticello, UT 84535. Phone: 801/587-2141.

Fremont Culture

In Utah about A.D. 900, many people began to live in somewhat the same way as the Anasazi farther south. Some archeologists call this Utah lifeway the Fremont culture and regard it as a subdivision of the Anasazi. Fremont people lived on the northern periphery of the Anasazi area and gathered wild foods, as their ancestors apparently had done for thousands of years, but they also raised corn. Unlike the Anasazi they wore moccasins rather than sandals. Much of their pottery was rather plain, and experts can easily distinguish it from Anasazi pottery, which was often more decorated. Like the Anasazi the Fremont people built dwellings of stone and adobe masonry.

In the eastern part of Utah the lifeway of the Fremont people differed somewhat from that of their neighbors in the western part, who are called Sevier (suh-VEER)-Fremont. Both the Fremont and the Sevier-Fremont left rock art on cliff walls throughout the area.

About A.D. 1100 the Fremont culture began to disappear. A recent theory suggests that Fremont people moved out of Utah, some to the south, where they merged with the ancestors of present-day Pueblos, some to the east, onto the Plains, probably through South Pass. According to this theory, which is based on cultural, skeletal, and linguistic evidence, the Shoshone Indians, whom the first white settlers found in Utah, were not descendants of the Fremont people but were fairly recent immigrants to the area.

One of many pictographs of figures without heads in Grand Gulch, Utah. Photo by Julia M. Johnson; copyright by Julia M. Johnson.

ARCHES NATIONAL PARK

From Moab drive 5 miles north on US 191 to Park Headquarters. Mail address: P.O. Box 907, Moab, UT 84532. Phone: 801/259-8161. Open daily, all year. Admission charged. Camping.

There are a number of pictograph and petroglyph sites in the park, the most accessible of which is the Courthouse Wash Panel. For directions to the site inquire at the Visitor Center. Some of the unusual paintings here are five feet or more tall, and are similar to paintings in Horseshoe Canyon (see entry below). On a portion of the same cliff are petroglyphs which have been carved into the sandstone. Unfortunately, because of its accessibility the site has been badly vandalized.

BARRIER CANYON

(See Horseshoe Canyon)

BEEF BASIN TOWERS

From the junction of US 191 and Utah 211, drive to Dugout Ranch on Utah 211, then 35 miles southwest on a gravel road that is open only during summer and fall. For detailed information apply at the Bureau of Land Management, San Juan Resource Area, 435 North Main St., P.O. Box 7, Monticello, UT 84535. Phone: 801/ 587-2141.

Here, in an area called Ruins Park, are numerous circular and square towers, some two stories high. There is also a small village site. Primitive trails lead to these structures that were built about the thirteenth century.

BRADFORD CANYON RUIN

For information about access, apply to Bureau of Land Management, San Juan Resource Area, 435 North Main St., P.O. Box 7, Monticello, UT 84535. Phone: 801/587-2141.

Here, on a series of terraces in a cliff, are granaries in caves and dwellings and surface ruins left by Anasazi peo-

Unlike most prehistoric structures in the Four Corners area, this one in Grand Gulch, Utah, was built, not of stone, but by the method called wattle and daub. The framework, made of woven branches, was then coated with mud. Photo by Julia M. Johnson; copyright by Julia M. Johnson.

ple in the eleventh century. Petroglyphs have been pecked in the nearby cliff face.

BRIGHAM YOUNG UNIVERSITY, MUSEUM OF PEOPLE AND CULTURE

710 N. 100 East, Provo, UT 84602 (off campus). Phone: 801/378-6112. Open free, Monday–Friday, September 1–May 1. Closed certain holidays.

This museum contains material of the Fremont culture in Utah, the Anasazi, the Hohokam, the Casas Grandes and the Mimbres cultures elesewhere in the Southwest.

BUTLER WASH OVERLOOK

From Blanding drive 15 miles west on Utah 95 to a turnout. Mail address: Bureau of Land Management, San Juan Resource Area, 435 North Main St., P.O. Box 7, Monticello, UT 84535. Phone: 801/587-2141.

From the turnout, a half-mile-long well-marked unpaved trail leads to 23 Anasazi structures from the mid-thir-

teenth century. At the site are restrooms, an interpretive sign and a nature guide brochure. Partially hidden nearby is a natural bridge.

BUTLER WASH PETROGLYPHS

Accessible by boat, 4 miles west of Bluff on the San Juan River. River travel permits for private boats are available from the Bureau of Land Management, Monticello, UT 84535. Phone: 801/672-2222.

Here are life-size rock carvings of human figures in a two-hundred-yard-long panel attributed to early Anasazi people. One-day commercial boat trips to the site are available, April 15–October 31. For information contact Wild Rivers Expeditions, P.O. Box 118, Bluff, UT 84512. Phone: 801/422-7654. Three- and four-day trips can also be arranged to visit this and other rock art sites along the San Juan River.

CANYONLANDS NATIONAL PARK

To reach the Island in the Sky district of the park, turn west from US 191, 11 miles north of Moab. To reach the Needles district, drive west on Utah 211. Other districts require a four-wheel drive vehicle. Mail address: National Park Service, Moab, UT 84532.

CALF CREEK RECREATION AREA

Along Utah 12, midway between Boulder and Escalante. Mail address: Bureau of Land Management, Escalante Resource Area, P.O. Box 225, Escalante, UT 84726. Phone: 801/826-4291. The office is on Utah 12 on the west edge of Escalante. Camping.

Several small Fremont-Anasazi ruins and pictographs are along 2.75 miles of the Lower Calf Creek Falls Trail. At the trailhead are interpretive brochures. There are also small ruins along Utah 12, 1.5 miles south of Calf Creek Campground near the Escalante River Bridge.

CAPITOL REEF NATIONAL PARK

On Utah 24, 75 miles southeast of the junction of Utah 24 with Interstate 70. Mail address: Torrey, UT 84775. Phone: 801/425-3791. Open daily. Closed certain holidays. Admission charged. Camping.

The Fremont people once lived in this area, and a portion of the Visitor Center is devoted to them. Petro-

glyphs and a great deal of their work has been preserved. Visitors may see both pictographs, which are paintings on rock and petroglyphs, which are pictures pecked or scraped into rock.

Throughout the park there are numerous small ruins of dwellings, granaries and kivas built by the Anasazi people between A.D. 900 and 1250. Visitors are invited to look at the ruins, but are forbidden to enter them. The rock walls of the canyons offered innumerable flat surfaces for prehistoric artists, and a great deal of their

2995. Phone: 801/259-7164. Open at all times. Admission charged. Primitive camping.

Prehistoric Indian rock art in Horse Canyon, Canyonlands National Park. National Park Service photo by N. Woodbridge Williams.

Handprints in Canyonlands National Park. National Park Service photo.

glyphs, probably made by Fremont people, may be seen near the highway.

CASTLE CREEK RUIN

From Utah 95 west of Blanding, drive 27 miles south on Utah 276. Mail address: Bureau of Land Management, San Juan Resource Area, 435 N. Main St., P.O. Box 7, Monticello, UT 84535. Phone: 801/587-2141.

Here against a cliff, between two springs, are several rooms connected by T-shaped doorways. A primitive trail from a turnout leads to the site.

CAVE CANYON TOWERS

Off Utah 95 in the Blanding area. For exact road directions contact the Bureau of Land Management, San Juan Resource Area, 435 N. Main St., P.O. Box 7, Monticello, UT 84535. Phone: 801/587-2141.

Here seven stone towers are clustered around a pool at the head of a canyon. Nearby are numerous rooms

built in various masonry styles that suggest occupation at different times. Not far away are other structures close to a group of petroglyphs, some of which may relate to solstice observation. Visitors are urged not to climb on or in the ruins.

CLEAR CREEK CANYON ROCK ART

Between Sevier and Cove Fort on Utah 44. Open free, at all times.

Many panels of petroglyphs may be seen along the walls of Clear Creek Canyon. The main concentration is between the mouths of Mill Creek and Dry Creek.

COLLEGE OF EASTERN UTAH PREHISTORIC MUSEUM

155 East Main, Price, UT 84501. Phone: 801/637-5060. Open Monday–Saturday. Closed certain holidays. Donations accepted.

The museum contains artifacts of the Fremont culture.

COTTONWOOD FALLS SITE

For information about access apply to Bureau of Land Management, San Juan Resource Area, 435 North Main St., P.O. Box 7, Monticello, UT 84535. Phone: 801/587-2141.

Here is a multistory Anasazi building with a nearby Great Kiva. A prehistoric roadway linked this site to others that are in present-day New Mexico.

Cliff dweller ruins on Westwater Creek near Blanding. Bureau of Land Management photo.

Anasazi people made their homes in areas such as this in Canyonlands National Park. National Park Service photo by George A. Grant.

Many small structures like this can be seen in protected areas in what is now Canyonlands National Park. National Park Service photo.

Prehistoric shields, made of buffalo hide, were found packed in juniper bark in a burial in the Capitol Reef National Park area. National Park Service photo by George A. Grant.

Petroglyphs in Capitol Reef National Park. National Park Service photo by Parker Hamilton.

COURTHOUSE WASH PANEL
(*See Arches National Park*)

DANGER CAVE STATE HISTORICAL SITE

One mile north of Wendover off US 40. For information write: Department of Natural Resources, Division of Parks and Recreation, 1636 W. North Temple, Salt Lake City, UT 84116. Phone: 801/533-4563.

This famous site, although so far undeveloped, has been opened to the public by the Utah Park system. For its significance see Introduction to Great Basin section.

Warning: Do not enter cave. The roof is unstable.

EDGE OF THE CEDARS STATE PARK

660 West 400 North, Blanding, UT 84511. Phone: 801/678-2238. Open daily. Closed certain holidays. Admission charged.

In the museum is a fine Anasazi pottery exhibit as well as exhibits of ma-

terial from prehistoric as well as historic Navajo and Ute cultures. Video presentations are available.

An Anasazi pueblo, dating from A.D. 800 to 1100, is located adjacent to the museum building.

FOUR CORNERS SCHOOL OF OUTDOOR EDUCATION

Mail address: East Route, Monticello, UT 84535. Phone: 1/800/525-4456 or 801/587-2859.

In addition to courses in the biology and history of the Colorado Plateau, the school offers numerous short courses in field archeology. A catalogue describes the courses that people may take at different times at important sites and excavations in all parts of the Four Corners region.

FREMONT INDIAN STATE PARK

Drive south from Richfield on Highway 89 to Clear Creek Junction. Go west on Interstate 70 for about five miles to the park. Mail address: 11550 Clear Creek Canyon Road, Sevier, UT

Edge of the Cedars Ruin, Blanding. Edge of the Cedars State Park.

84766. Phone: 801/527-4631. Open daily. Closed certain holidays. Admission charged. Camping.

In the Visitor Center a video program and exhibits introduce visitors to the Fremont people. Three trails lead to pictographs and petroglyphs. One trail is concrete and wheel chair accessible. There is also a self-guided auto trail. Possibly visitors may be able to observe archeologists at work in an excavation.

GOULDINGS

At just about the point where US 191 crosses the border between Arizona and Utah, 24 miles north of Kayenta, drive west 3 miles on a local road. A small museum here exhibits some prehistoric artifacts.

Although its post office address is in Utah, this trading post and motel has long been associated with Navajoland in Arizona. Visitors who want to see prehistoric sites in Monument Valley can arrange for guided, four-wheel-drive day or half-day trips. For information, from April–November,

write to Box 1, Monument Valley, Utah 84536. Phone: 801/727-3231.

GRAND GULCH

From Blanding drive south on US 191, then 35 miles southwest on Utah 95 to intersection with Utah 261, then 4 miles south on Utah 261 to Kane Gulch. A hiking trail leads down Kane Gulch to Grand Gulch, about a two-hour trip. Visitors who want to see a representative sample of Grand Gulch sites should plan to spend three days. The entire length of the Gulch is 52 miles. Open free, for day hikes. A fee is charged for overnight or longer. Visitors must register at the Kane Gulch Ranger Station and must carry drinking water.

This is a deep canyon, rich in archeological remains, with many large, well-preserved Anasazi dwellings. There are three major hiking trails into the Grand Gulch. Anyone interested in guide service should apply to the Bureau of Land Management, P.O. Box 7, Monticello, UT 84535. Phone: 801/587-2141.

HOG SPRINGS PICNIC SITE

From Hanksville drive 37 miles south on Utah 95. Open at all times. Admission charged.

Near the picnic site is a rock shelter containing Indian pictographs, one of which is called the Moki Queen by local residents. Administered by the Bureau of Land Management.

HORSESHOE CANYON
(Barrier Canyon)

Accessible only by four-wheel drive vehicle and foot trail. From Green River drive 9 miles west on Interstate 70 to Utah 24, then south to sign for Goblin Valley State Park; continue to unimproved dirt road (next left), and follow Maze district signs to Hans Flat Ranger Station, where further directions to the canyon can be obtained. Mail address: National Park Service, Southeast Utah Group, Moab, UT 84532-2995. Phone: 801/259-7164.

Throughout Horseshoe Canyon are large paintings of human figures on sandstone cliff walls. These may have been made by Archaic hunter-gatherers who inhabited the area from 6000 B.C. to A.D. 1.

ogy.

In a cave in the Grand Gulch, Richard found, underneath layers of dust and debris containing things left by Pueblo people, artifacts made by Basketmaker people. This surely meant, said Wetherill, that the Basketmakers lived in the Southwest earlier than the Pueblos. Today the idea seems obvious, but at that time American archeologists had not made use of the principle of stratigraphy (the study of strata or layers in the earth), which had long been used in European archeology.

Pottery from Grand Gulch is now in the Field Museum of Natural History, Chicago; Smithsonian Institution, Washington, DC; University Museum, Philadelphia; and Hearst Museum, Berkeley. It was collected in part by Richard Wetherill, a member of a Quaker family who settled near Mancos, Colorado, in the 1880s. From the home ranch he and his brothers, John and Clayton, went out on many exploring expeditions and made many archeological discoveries.

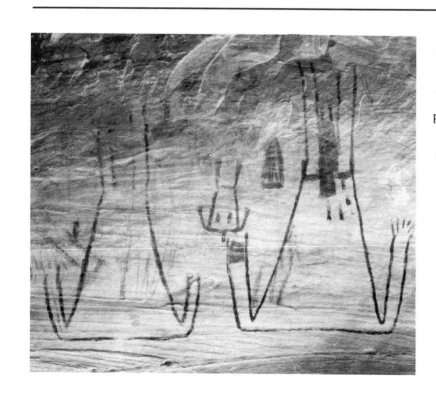

Breech birth, a rare pictograph in Grand Gulch. It is part of a panel in an alcove with one called the Green Mask which intrigues archeologists because it depicts a face, also painted in green, on a mask made of human skin that was found elsewhere in the region. The original mask was not cared for properly and has disintegrated. Photo by Bob Powell, copyright, Bob Powell.

Part of a group of pictographs known as Big Man Panel in Grand Gulch, Utah. Photo by Julia M. Johnson; copyright by Julia M. Johnson.

An unusual tipi-shaped structure in an alcove in Grand Gulch, Utah. Photo by Julia M. Johnson; copyright by Julia M. Johnson.

HOVENWEEP NATIONAL MONUMENT

From Cortez, Colorado, drive north 18 miles on US 666 to Pleasant View; turn west at the Hovenweep directional sign and follow the graded road 27.2 miles to Square Tower Group, which is in Utah. Mail address: Mesa Verde National Park, CO 81330. Phone: 801/529-4465. Open free, all year. Camping.

In this extremely isolated spot are imposing and well-preserved towers and other structures built by people who followed about the same lifeway as the ancient farmers of Mesa Verde. Exact dates and many details about the Hovenweep people are not yet known, because there has been no excavation at this site. Visitors take self-guided tours on a number of trails leading to the most interesting of the ruins. A ranger on duty at the Visitor Center will answer questions.

The Name. On September 13, 1874, a party exploring for the United States government camped at this place. Ernest Ingersoll, a zoologist, and W. H. Jackson, a photographer, were members of the expedition. Ingersoll noted in his journal that the place was named by the explorers from two Indian words meaning "deserted canyon."

Special Feature. Hovenweep is a kind of bank in which archeological riches are being kept for future generations of scientists to excavate and study. Archeologists approve this policy, because new techniques are constantly being developed, which make it possible to learn more and more from the materials recovered at a site. When Hovenweep is excavated in the future, it will yield information that might be lost if digging went on today. Once a site is excavated it is destroyed as a source of scientific information.

LITTLE BLACK MOUNTAIN PETROGLYPH INTERPRETIVE SITE

Eight miles southeast of St. George. Four-wheel-drive vehicle recommended. For road directions inquire at Bureau of Land Management, Shivwits Resource Area, 225 N. Bluff, St. George, UT 84770. Phone: 801/628-4491.

About 500 designs or design elements appear here in an area 800 yards long on cliffs and boulders. Many different groups who traveled and traded through the area left this art work. Visitors are asked to stay on the trails and not to touch any of the petroglyphs.

Detail showing masonry of round towers at Hovenweep National Monument.

Above and opposite: Many towers at Hovenweep National Monument are square. Others are circular or oval or D-shaped. Until scientific excavation is done, there can only be speculation about the meaning and use of the towers. However, it is known that one of the towers has an opening suitable for marking the summer and winter solstices. National Park Service photo by Fred E. Mang, Jr.

MULE CANYON INDIAN RUINS

From Blanding drive south on US 191, then west 20 miles on Utah 95. Mail address: Bureau of Land Management, P.O. Box 7, Monticello, UT 84535. Phone: 801/587-2141. Open free, all year.

This site was discovered and excavated during a survey prior to the construction of the new Utah 95. After the ruins were stabilized, the Bureau of Land Management built trails, restrooms and a protective shelter over one structure.

Anasazi people lived here shortly before A.D. 1300. The small complex consists of rooms for dwelling and storage, a kiva and a tower that might have been used for defense or as a platform for sending signals with fire or smoke. A crawlway led from the kiva to one of the house rooms. The site was probably the home of an extended family of about eight adults and their children.

NAMPAWEAP

For road directions apply to Bureau of Land Management, Vermillion Resource Area, 225 N. Bluff, St. George, UT 85770. Phone: 801/628-4491.

At this site are hundreds of petroglyphs. Nampaweap means "foot canyon" in the Paiute language.

NATURAL BRIDGES NATIONAL MONUMENT

From Blanding drive 40 miles west on Utah 95. Mail address: Box 1, Natural Bridges, Lake Powell, UT 84533. Phone: 801/259-5174. Open all year. Trails may be closed during winter. Admission charged in summer. Camping.

Within the monument are 200 sites once occupied by Anasazi people. Hikers who follow the trails will pass a cliff dwelling with several rooms, granaries, and kivas, which may be viewed but not entered. Federal laws protecting antiquities are enforced.

NEWSPAPER ROCK STATE PARK

Drive 12 miles north of Monticello on US 191, then 12 miles west on Utah 211 to Indian Creek where one of the most easily accessible rock art panels is located. Phone: 801/678-2238. Open free, all year. Camping.

Here a large cliff wall is covered with Indian rock art that may have accumulated over a period of 1,500 years. It seems likely that the more recent petroglyphs were made by historic Ute Indians, but visible under them and around the edges are much older petroglyphs made by the Fremont and Anasazi people between A.D. 800 and 1300.

NINE MILE CANYON ROCK ART

Between Price and Myton on Utah 53. Open free, at all times.

Many rock-art panels are visible along the walls of this canyon. Occasional granaries and other structures, attributed to the Fremont culture, may also be seen. Before starting this trip be sure to have gasoline and drinking water.

The symbols on this stone slab, called Newspaper Rock, may have had real meaning to the people who put them there, but experts agree that they do not constitute true writing. The symbols cover an area 25 feet long and 25 feet high in Indian Creek State Park. Photo by Norman Van Pelt.

PAROWAN GAP INDIAN DRAWINGS
(pair-oh-WAN)

From Cedar City drive north 18 miles on Interstate 15 to Parowan turnoff, then west on county road toward Utah 130. The site is next to the road. Open free, at all times. Phone: 801/586-2458. Camping nearby.

Drawings and designs seem to have been placed on the rock here by the Fremont people sometime between A.D. 900 and 1150. Administered by the Bureau of Land Management, Grand Resource Area, 885 S. Sand Flats Road, Moab, UT 84532. Phone: 801/259-8193.

POTASH ROAD PETROGLYPHS

From Moab drive 8 miles west on Utah 279. Mail address: Bureau of Land Management, Grand Resource Area, S. Sand Flats Road, P.O. Box M, Moab, UT 88532. Phone: 801/259-8193.

Rock art panels line the sheer cliffs on the north side of the highway for two miles. The panels include a variety of art styles and subjects. Artists made these panels from the Archaic period through the Pueblo to the days of the Ute.

RIVER HOUSE RUIN

For directions to this site near Bluff, apply to the Bureau of Land Management, San Juan Resource Area, 435 N. Main St., P.O. Box 7, Monticello, UT 84535. Phone: 801/587-2141.

This site, in a sandstone alcove, overlooks the San Juan River. In it are 14 rooms, some two stories tall, that date from the thirteenth century.

SAND ISLAND PETROGLYPHS

From Bluff drive 2 miles southwest on US 191 to directional marker. Open free, at all times. Camping.

A large panel of petroglyphs, protected by a wire fence, overlooks the San Juan River. The carvings of animals, human beings and abstract designs probably date back to Anasazi times. One of the figures is that of Kokopelli, the humpbacked flute player, who appeared frequently in Southwestern rock art. His exact significance is not known. Some interpret him as a trader, possibly with a pack on his back. Others believe he was a fertility figure.

SEGO CANYON PETROGLYPHS
(*See Thompson Wash Petroglyphs*)

SHAY CANYON PETROGLYPHS

From Monticello drive north on US 191, then 12 miles west on Utah 211 to a turnout. From here the site, 100 yards distant, is reached by a primitive trail. Mail address: Bureau of Land Management, San Juan Resource Area, 435 North Main St., P.O. Box 7, Monticello, UT 84535. Phone: 801/587-2141.

Here on towering sandstone cliffs is rock art in a great variety of styles and motifs. Prominent are Kokopelli figures.

SOUTH FORK INDIAN CANYON PICTOGRAPH SITE

Near Coral Pink Sand Dunes State Park, near Kanab. For exact road directions inquire at the Bureau of Land Management, Kanab Resource Area, P.O. Box 459, Kanab, UT 84741. Phone: 801/644-2672. For four-wheel drive vehicles only. At the end of the drive there is a twenty-minute walk. Open free, at all times. Camping nearby.

This site is a high-roofed, spacious rock shelter located well below the rim of a major tributary of scenic Cottonwood Canyon, one of the large, deeply cut drainages coming off the tablelands north and west of Kanab. On the sandstone shelter walls are numerous painted figures of people and animals, in addition to several more abstract elements. Some previously covered figures have been exposed by looters digging along the rear wall.

The badly vandalized deposits of the shelter contain large quantities of corn cobs and show some evidence of stone-lined storage cists with covers of small logs (a section of a log yielded a C-14 date of ca. A.D. 280). The site appears to be quite similar to a Basketmaker II site, Cave Du Pont, located just a few miles to the north. The pictographs are also taken to date from this early agricultural period.

Weather Prediction

Archeologists have developed many strategies for determining what the weather was like at various periods in the past—and how it affected the lives of Native Americans. Growth rings in trees, for example, reflect periods of drought and heavy rainfall which brought bad or good crops. The remains of various types of vegetation in layers of earth, which geologists can date, indicate whether plants that were tolerant of cool and dry or warm and wet weather were flourishing at one period or another.

Certain snails proliferate in wet climates, others in dry. By determining which type is found in a particular layer of earth associated with human remains, an archeologist can tell whether much or little rain fell on the people who lived there.

Most archeologists have theorized that from about 8000 B.C. to 4000 B.C. the weather in the Southwest was cool and dry. This notion has been challenged by an ingenious method of linking climate to the remains of the meat that people ate. Analysis of the faunal bones found in caves used by hunters in the Southwest indicate that many of these same animals now exist only in warmer, wetter environments to the north and east of the caves. Therefore, it is assumed, the Southwest in ancient times must have been warmer and wetter than it is now, and so was more attractive to hunters than archeologists previously thought.

THOMPSON WASH PETROGLYPHS

From Thompson drive 3.4 miles north on a local road. The site is marked on Utah highway maps as "Sego Canyon Petroglyphs." Mail address: Bureau of Land Management, Grand Resource Area, 885 S. Sand Flats Road, Moab, UT 84532. Phone: 801/259-8193. Open free, at all times.

There are extensive panels of both carving and painting on the rocks in this area. This rock art comes from three different cultures and three different time periods.

THREE KIVA PUEBLO

From Monticello drive south on US 191 about 4 miles to Montezuma Canyon Rd., then 3 miles into the canyon to an interpretive sign. Four-wheel-drive vehicle recommended because of deep sand in places. For information inquire at Monticello office of the Bureau of Land Management. Phone: 801/587-2141.

This village, the ruins of which have been stabilized, was occupied at least three different times from A.D. 900 to 1300. Close to the dwellings is an area that archeologists believe was a turkey pen.

UNIVERSITY OF UTAH, UTAH MUSEUM OF NATURAL HISTORY

On the campus, Wasatch Drive, Salt Lake City. Phone: 801/581-4303. Open daily. Admission charged.

Archeological exhibits in this museum include dioramas and materials from the important excavations at Hogup Cave and Danger Cave. For the story of Danger Cave, see Introduction to Great Basin section and entry above.

UTAH FIELD HOUSE OF NATURAL HISTORY STATE PARK

235 East Main St., Vernal, UT 84078. Phone: 801/789-3799. Open daily. Closed certain holidays. Admission charged.

Within this natural history mu-

Diorama showing what a prehistoric village, now in ruins, may have looked like when people lived in Zion National Park. National Park Service photo.

seum are displays of prehistoric artifacts. The cultures represented are primarily the Fremont, Basketmaker and Ute Indian.

UTAH MUSEUM OF NATURAL HISTORY
(*See University of Utah*)

WESTWATER FIVE KIVA RUIN

From the center of Blanding drive south on US Highway 191 2 miles, to the Scenic View 2 sign, turn right and follow to the end of the pavement, 2 miles. Mail address: Department of Natural Resources, P.O. Box 788, Blanding, UT 84511. Phone: 801/678-2238. Open free, daily, all year

Westwater Five Kiva ruin is an Anasazi cliff dwelling located across Westwater Canyon. It was occupied from about A.D. 1150 to1275. It consists of several living rooms, five kivas, storage rooms and open area.

WHITE MESA INSTITUTE

College of Eastern Utah, San Juan Campus, Blanding, UT. Mail address: P.O. Box 211248, Salt Lake City, UT 84121-8248. Phone (at the college): 801/678-2201.

This Institute offers lectures on archeology and expeditions to a variety of archeological sites and areas. In addition there are opportunities to take part in excavation.

ZION NATIONAL PARK

From Kanab (kah-NAB) drive 17 miles north on US 89, then 24 miles west on Utah 9 to Park Headquarters. Mail address: Springdale, UT 84767. Phone: 801/772-3256. Open daily. Admission charged.

The deep canyons and towering cliffs of this area were known to ancient Basketmaker and Pueblo people. A number of sites have been excavated, but none have been prepared for the public. An archeological diorama in the Visitor Center museum depicts prehistoric settlements in the park.

STATE ARCHEOLOGISTS

Arizona
Paul Fish
Curator of Archaeology
Arizona State Museum
University of Arizona
Tucson AZ 85721
602/621-2556
602/323-0800

New Mexico
Dr. Lynn Sebastian
State Archaeologist
Historic Preservation Div.
Villa Rivera Bldg.
228 E. Palace Ave.
Santa Fe, NM 87503
505/827-6320

Colorado
Susan M. Collins
State Archaeologist
Colorado Historical Society
1300 Broadway
Denver, CO 80203
303/866-2736

Utah
David B. Madsen
State Archaeologist
Division of State History
300 Rio Grande
Salt Lake City, UT 84101
801/533-4563

INDEX

Abo, 67

Acoma Pueblo, 67

Agate House, 34

agriculture: corn, 3–5; cotton, 27, 63; domestication of plants, 3, 4, 26; general development, 26; grid gardens, 93; irrigation, 5, 18, 27, 35, 55, 60, 84, and salt damage, 35; Southwest, 3–4, 42–43

Aleuts, 15

Alkali Ridge, 107

amateurs, 44. *See also* field schools; visiting excavations; volunteering

Amerind Foundation, Inc., 15

Anasazi culture: classified, 46; described, 4, 7–10, 30; discussed, 54–61, 78–86; mentioned, 7, 16–17, 21, 25, 28, 30, 37, 43, 46, 47, 51, 55, 64, 71, 78, 86, 87, 93, 94, 107–11 passim, 114, 120, 121, 123; settlements at Aztec Ruins, 68,

Bandelier, 71–74, Chimney Rock, 47, Dominguez and Escalante, 51–52, Glen Canyon, 21, Grand Canyon, 21, Kinlichee, 25, Montezuma Castle, 27, Petrified Forest, 34, Wupatki, 43

Anasazi Heritage Center, 47, 50

Anasazi Indian Village State Park, 107

Anasazi National Park, 46

Anderson, C. W., 76

Antiquities Act, 44

Apache Indians, 15, 40, 77, 91

Arch Canyon Ruin, 107

Archaeological Investigations at Chimney Rock Mesa 1970–72, 40

Archaic culture: 26; Southwest, 26, 116; Western, 50, 116

Archeoastronomy, 48, 64, 85, 119; astronomical devices, 85

Arches National Park, 108

Architecture: adobe buildings, 86,

88, and caliche, 19; Anasazi, 8, 9, 17, 26, 56, 68, 71, 78, 79, 80, 81; Basketmaker, 8; Chaco Outliers, 47, 48, 50–51, 53, 68, 101; cliff dwellings, 71, 99; Hohokam, 5–6, 18, 19, 26–27, at Casa Grande, 18; ladders and screens, 69; masonry, 9, 80, 81, 86, 87, 118; Mogollon, 5, 91; pithouses, 5, 8, 20, 36, 41, 56, 58, 81, 90, 92; Puebloan, 9, 17, 26, 40, 47–53, 55–61, 68, 71, 78–81, 86, 92, 95, 99, 101, 103; wattle and daub, 7, 49, 50, 109, 117. *See also* Cliff dwellings; Kivas; Mounds; village development

Arizona, 15–43

Arizona State Museum, University of Arizona, 40

Arizona State University, Museum of Anthropology, 15

A:Shiwi A:Wan Museum, 105

Athabascan language, 145
Awatovi, 98
"Ax, Adze, and Celt," 6
Aztec Ruins National Monument, 9, 68, 69, 82, 84

Balcony House, 59
ball courts, 6, 35, 42, 43
"Ball Courts," 43
Bandelier, Adolph, 74, 96
Bandelier National Monument, 71–74
Barrier Canyon, 108
Basketmakers, 8, 9, 46, 56, 81, 107, 116, 121, 123
basketry, 56
Beef Basin Towers, 108
Bering Land Bridge, 15, 89
Besh-Ba-Gowah Archeological Park, 16
Betatakin, 29, 30, 32
Big Man Panel, 117
Black Cowboy: The Life and Legend of George McJunkin, 88
black explorer, 105
Blackwater Draw Museum, 74
Blackwater Draw Site, 74–6
bones, animal, study of, 122
Bradford Canyon Ruin, 108
Brew, J.O., 107
Brigham Young University, Museum of People and Culture, 109
Bright Angel Pueblo, 22
Browns Park, 51
Bureau of Land Management, 46, 47, 53, 61, 64, 77, 115, 116
Butler Wash Overlook, 109
Butler Wash Petroglyphs, 109

C-14 dating: described, 12–13; mentioned, 22, 50, 121
Cabeza de Vaca, 105
Calf Creek Recreation Area, 110
canals, 18
Canyon de Chelly National Monument, 8, 12, 16–17, 24
Canyon Pintado Historical District, 46, 61

Canyonlands National Park, 110, 111, 113
Cape Royal Ruin, 22
Capitol Reef National Park, 110, 114
Capulin Volcano, 76
"Carbon-14 Dating," 12–13. *See also* C-14 dating
Carling Reservoir Site, 17
Carlsbad Caverns National Park, 76, 77
Carson, Christopher "Kit," 17, 94
Casa Grande Ruins National Monument, 17, 18, 19
Casa Malpais, 18
Casa Rinconada, 66, 78, 86
Casamero Ruins, 77
Casas Grandes, Mexico, 5, 94, 104, 109
Castle Creek Ruin, 111
catlinite, 25
Cave Du Pont, 121
cave dwellers, 8; and caves, 21, 29, 71, 73, 74, 75, 77, 90, 91, 98, 113, 117. *See also* caves by name
cave paintings, 17
Cave Towers, 111
caves by name: Goat, 77; Painted Grotto, 77; Sandia Man, 101; Ventana, 41
Cedar Tree Tower, 59–60
Center of Southwest Studies, 46
ceremonial centers, 18, 26, 48, 58, 68, 86
ceremonial practices: Anasazi, 65; Ball game, 6; Basketmaker, 9; burial, 9; Dance platform, 23, 67; Harvest, 4; healing/curing, 60; kachina, 33, kivas, 57–58, 68, 96; shamans, 105; Snake Dance, 42; others, 86
Chaco Canyon: discussed, 78–86; mentioned, 10, 30, 47, 48; Outliers listed, 84
Chaco Culture National Historical Park, 78–86
Chaco Outliers by name; Aztec, 68; Casamero, 77; Chimney Rock,

48; Dominguez and Escalante, 51–52; Lowry, 53; Salmon Ruin, 101; Village of the Great Kivas, 105
Chama Gateway Pueblos, 90
Chetro Ketl, 78, 79
Chimney Rock, 47–48, 49, 84
"Classifying Anasazi Culture," 46
Clear Creek Canyon Rock Art, 111
Cliff Dwellings, 2, 12, 16, 26, 27, 29–32, 37, 38, 39, 41, 54–61, 64, 70–75, 90, 91, 112, 120; Cave dwellers, 8
Cliff Palace, 54, 56, 58, 59, 60, 61
Clovis Points, 28, 29, 76, 88, 89
Cochise culture, 4, 5, 6
Cochiti Pueblo, 71
Coconino National Forest, 20
Cohonina Culture, 23
College of Eastern Utah, Prehistoric Museum, 111
Colonies: *See* Chaco Canyon: Outliers listed
Colorado: southwestern, 46–64
Colorado National Monument, 48
Colorado Plateau, 114
Colorado River, 6–7, 21, 22
cooking practices: boiling stones, 56; mano-metate grinding, 11; roasting pits, 20, 76
Coombs Site, 107
Copper artifacts, 5, 81
corn. *See* agriculture: corn
Coronado, Francisco Vasquez de, 95, 105
Coronado State Monument, 86
Cortez CU Center, 46, 50
Cottonwood Falls Site, 111
"Could a Clovis Point Kill a Mammoth?" 28
Courthouse Wash Panel, 108
Coze, Paul, 71
Cross Canyon Ruins, 25
Crow Canyon Archaeological Center, 50
Cummings, Byron, 30
Curecanti National Recreation Area, 50–51

Danger Cave, 122
Danger Cave State Historical Site, 114
dating methods: relative or stratigraphic, 116; tree-ring, 33, 101, 106; *See also* C-14 dating
Delight Makers, The, 74
dendrochronology, 106
desiccated body, 9
diffusion, 3, 4, 5, 6
Dinosaur Natural History Museum, 51
Dittert Site, 87
dogs, 25; dog hair fabric, 25, 26
"Dogs and Prehistoric Americans," 25
Dolores Project, 46
Dominguez and Escalante Ruins, 51–52, 84
Dry Creek, 111

Early Man, 26, 89. *See also* Paleo-Indians
Earthwatch, 26
Eastern Arizona College, 19
Eastern Arizona Museum, 19
Echo House, 7
Eddy, Frank W., 49
Edge of the Cedars State Park, 114, 115
education. *See* field schools; hands-on exhibits; visiting excavations
effigies: pottery, 15, 25, 62
Elden Pueblo, 20
Ellis, Florence Hawley, 88
El Morro National Monument, 87
engineering: at Mesa Verde, 60
Ernest Thompson Seton Museum, 87
Escalante Ruin, 47, 50, 51, 52, 84
Eskimos, 15
Euler, Robert, 21

"Fanciful Archeology," 101
Far View Ruins, 60, 61
field schools, 24, 101, 114
figurines, 22
Five Kiva House, 123

Florence Hawley Ellis Museum of Anthropology, 88
"Fluted Points," 89
Folsom Man State Monument, 76
Folsom Museum, 88
Folsom points, 52, 76, 88, 89
Folsom Site, 88
Fort Lewis College, 46
Fort Lowell Museum, 20, 24
Four Corners area, defined, 17; mentioned, 100, 109, 114
Four Corners School of Outdoor Education, 114
Franciscans, 52, 93, 96
"Fremont Culture," 108
Fremont culture and people, 46, 48, 51, 61, 108, 109, 110, 111, 115, 120, 121, 123
Fremont Indian State Park, 114
Frijoles Canyon, 71, 74
Frison, George C., 28

Gallina culture, 88
games: ball, 6, 35, 43
Gatlin Site, 20
Geronimo Springs Museum, 90
Ghost Ranch Living Museum, 90
Gila Bend Museum, 20
Gila Cliff Dwelling National Monument, 90–91
Gila Pueblo, 19, 20
Gila River, 5, 18, 28
Giusewa, 93
Gladwin, Harold, and Winifred Gladwin, 20
Glen Canyon National Recreation Area, 21
Gouldings, 115
Gran Chichimeca, 22
Gran Quivira, 67, 92
Grand Canyon National Park, 21–23
Grand Gulch, 108, 109, 115, 116, 117
Grasshopper Ruin, 24
grave goods, 52
grave robbers, 44
Great Basin and California, 124

great kivas, 19, 50, 51, 53, 67, 68, 77, 79, 84, 86, 87, 101, 105, 111
Great Sand Dunes National Monument, 52–53
"Grizzlier than Grizzlies," 97
Guadalupe Ruin, 92
Gunnison River, 50

handicapped access, 16, 47, 104, 115
hand-on exhibits, 28, 46, 50
Hans Flat Ranger District, 116
Hardy Site, 20, 24
Haury, Emil, 41
Havasupai Indians, 7, 23
Hawikuh, 92, 105
Heard Museum, 24
"Heritage and Landmark Sites," 36
"History of Prehistory, The," 89
Hog Springs Picnic Site, 116
Hogup Cave, 122
Hohokam Culture, 4, 5–6, 15, 18, 19, 20, 26, 27, 33, 34–35, 37, 40, 41, 43, 109
Homolovi Ruins State Park, 24
Hopi Indians, 21, 24, 28, 33, 40, 42, 56
Horse Canyon, 110
Horseshoe Canyon, 108, 116
household activities. *See* cooking practices; personal adornment; women's activities
Hovenweep National Monument, 118, 119
Howard, Edgar B., 76
Humpbacked flute player, 121; *see also* Kokopelli
hunting, 102; mammoth, 28, 41
Hupobi ruin, 93

Ice Age, 28. *See also* Early Man; Paleo-Indians
Indian Creek State Park, 120
Ingersoll, Ernest, 118
Inscription House, 30, 31
interdisciplinary studies, 85
Inter-Tribal Ceremonial, 100

Irwin-Williams, Cynthia, 101, 104
Island in the Sky District of
    Canyonlands, 110

Jackson, W. H., 118
Jemez Pueblo, 93, 96
Jemez Rangers, 93
Jemez State Monument, 93
Johnson Canyon, 64
Jornada Branch of Mogollon
    Culture, 104

"Kachinas," 33
Kane Gulch, 115
Kayenta Anasazi, 10, 30
Keet Seel, 24, 29, 31
Kidder, A. V., 96
Kill Sites; mammoth, 41
Kinishba Pueblo, 25
Kinlichee Tribal Park, 25–26
Kino, Father, 18
Kit Carson Historic Museum, 94
kivas: construction, 57; history, 58;
    painted, 53, 86; plans for, 65;
    tower, 101; mentioned, 33, 47,
    48, 50, 53, 59, 60, 61, 66, 68,
    73, 79, 83, 92, 96, 98, 105,
    107, 110, 120, 122. See also
    great kivas
Kokopelli, 24
Koster Site, 25
Kuaua, 86

Laboratory of Anthropology, 94
Lake Powell, 21
legislation to support archeology, 44
Lehner site, 41, 89
Lister, Robert H., 83
Little Black Mountain Petroglyph,
    118
Little Colorado River, 18
Long House, 55
Los Alamos Historical Museum, 94
Lovato, Ike, 93
Lowry Pueblo Ruins, 53

macaws, 5, 9, 81
Many Cherries Canyon, 24

Marana Mound, 26
Maricopa Indians, 7
Mason, Charles, 59, 60
Maxwell, Dorothy, and Gilbert
    Maxwell, 104
Maxwell Museum of Anthropology,
    94
McJunkin, George, 88
McPhee Reservoir, 46
Mesa Southwest Museum, 26
Mesa Verde National Park, dis-
    cussed, 54, 55–61, 62, 63;
    mentioned, 8, 10, 30, 37, 51–
    52, 64, 68, 101, 118
Mexico, 3, 4, 5, 6, 22, 35
migrations, 15, 17, 22, 27, 30, 37–
    38, 40, 41, 53, 56, 68, 81, 84,
    99, 101
Mill Creek culture, 111
Millicent Rogers Museum, 94
Mimbres culture (pottery), 5, 39,
    61, 94, 104, 109
Mimbres River, 5
mining, 20
Missions, Spanish, 67, 92, 93, 99
Mississippian culture, mentioned,
    25
Mogollon-Anasazi pueblo, 25
Mogollon culture, 4–5, 18, 25, 41,
    43, 45, 90, 91, 92, 94, 104
Mojave Indians, 39
Moki Queen, 116
Montezuma Castle National
    Monument, 2, 26–27, 40, 65
Montezuma Well, 26, 27
Monument Valley, 28, 115
Monument Valley Tribal Park, 28
Morfield Campground, 61
Morris, Earl, 68
Mounds: platform, 34; pyramid, 35
Mug House, 61
Muller-Beck, H., 89
Mummy Lake, 60
Murray Springs Clovis Site, 28
Museum of Anthropology, Eastern
    Arizona College, 28
Museum of Indian Arts and
    Culture, 94

Museum of New Mexico, 93, 95
Museum of Northern Arizona, 28
Museum of People and Culture,
    Brigham Young University, 109
Museum of Western Colorado, 61

Naco Site, 41
National Forests, 20, 97
National Historic Landmarks, 20,
    36
National Landmark Site, 18
National Register of Historic Places,
    39
Navajo Community College, 29
Navajo Indians, 8, 15, 16, 17, 25,
    28, 114
Navajo National Monument, 10,
    29–30, 31, 32
Navajo Tribal Museum, 30
Ned Hatathli Center, 29
Needles District of Canyonlands,
    110
New Mexico, 67–105
New Mexico State University
    Museum, 94
Newspaper Rock, Arizona, 34
Newspaper Rock Petroglyphs, 33
Newspaper Rock State Park, 120
Newspaper Rock, Utah, 120
Nine Mile Canyon Rock Art, 120
Nokachok Kachina doll, 33

Obelisk Cave, 56
Old Oraibi, 33
Oraibi Pueblo, 33
Oshara Tradition, 8
overpopulation, 48, 52, 68, 84

painted caves, 17, 74, 75, 77
Painted Desert Visitor Center, 34
Painted Grotto, 77
Painted Hand Pueblo, 61
Painted kiva, 53, 98
Painted Rocks State park, 33
Paiute language, 120
Pajarito Plateau, 71, 94, 95, 103
Palace of the Governors, 94–95
"Paleo and Archaic," 26

Paleo-Indians: origin of, 15; mentioned, 28, 40, 97
Papago Indians, 6, 35
Park of the Canals, 33
Parowan Gap Indian Drawings, 121
Patayan culture, 4, 6–7, 23
Pecos Classification, 46
Pecos Conference, 96
Pecos Indians, 95–96
Pecos National Historical Park, 95–96
Pecos River, 95
Pecos, Virginia, Ms., 95
Peopling of the Americas, 15
personal adornment: cradles and head shaping, 46; hair brush, 13; *see also* grave goods
Petrified Forest National Park, 34, 35
Petroforms; Topoc Maze, 39
Petroglyph National Monument, 96
petroglyphs, in Arizona, 21, 34, 35; Colorado, 61, 64; New Mexico, 84, 87, 96, 104; Utah, 107, 108, 109, 111, 118, 120, 121, 122; the meaning of, 21, 51, 110
Philmont Scout Ranch, 103
Pictograph Point, 61
pictographs, in Arizona, 17, 21, 33; Colorado, 53, 61; New Mexico, 74, 75, 77; Utah, 108, 109, 111, 116, 121; the meaning of, 21, 51, 110
Picture Rocks Retreat, 34
Picuris Pueblo, 97
Pima Indians, 6, 35
Pimeria Alta Museum, 34
Piro Indians, 67
Plains Indians, 95
Point Sublime, 23
points. *See* tools
Poshu Uinge, 97
Potash Road Petroglyphs, 121
"Pot Hound and Grave Robber," 44
potterymaking, 5, 64
"Prehistoric Astronomers," 85
"Prehistoric Cosmology," 65
"Prehistoric Firepower," 102

Pueblo Alto, 86
Pueblo Bonito, 78, 83, 86
Pueblo culture, 9, 26, 28, 87, 90, 95, 116, 123; classified, 96
Pueblo del Arroyo, 78
Pueblo Grande Museum, 34–35
Pueblo Indians, 16, 33, 52, 88, 90. *See also* Pueblo Culture
Puerco Indian Ruins, 34
Puye Cliff Ruins, 98, 99, 103
pyramids. *See* Mounds: pyramid

Quarai, 99

Rangeley Museum, 61, 64
reconstructions, 21, 26, 68, 86
Red Rock State Park Museum, 100
Redemptorist Fathers, 34
religion. *See* "Prehistoric Cosmology"
religious practices. *See* ceremonial practices
restorations. *See* reconstructions
revolt of Pueblo Indians, 96
Rio Grande (Valley), 56, 67, 86, 88, 92
Rito de los Frijoles, 71
River House Ruin, 121
roads from Chaco Canyon, 64, 81–84, 111
Roberts, George, 76
rock art, 17, 21, 33, 34, 35, 51, 64, 74, 77, 84, 87, 96, 104, 108, 111, 116, 120. *See also* petroforms, petroglyphs, pictographs
Rock Art of the Painted Canyon, 64
rock shelter, 61. *See also* caves
Ruins Road, 58–61

Salado culture and peoples, 16, 19, 20, 26, 37, 39
Salinas National Monument, 67, 92, 99, 100
Salmon, George, 101
Salmon Ruin, 82, 84, 100–101
Salt Lake, Zuni, 105
Salt River, 5, 37

Salt River Valley, 26, 33, 39
salvage archeology, 46, 77
San Ildefonso Pueblo, 74
San Jose de los Jemez, 93
San Juan County Archeology Center and Museum, 101
San Juan National Forest, Pagosa Ranger District, 47
San Juan Pueblo, 88, 103
San Juan River, 109, 121
San Luis Valley, 52
San Pedro River, 5
San Pedro River Valley, 41
Sand and East Rock Canyons, 64
Sand Dune Pony, 53
Sand Island (Petroglyphs), 107, 121
sand paintings, 29
Sandia Man Cave, 101
Sandia points, 101
Santa Clara Pueblo, 98, 99, 103
Sapawe Pueblo, 88
Sego Canyon Petroglyphs, 121
Seton Museum, 103
Sevier Fremont Culture, 108
Sharlot Hall Museum, 36
Shay Canyon Petroglyphs, 121
Shoshone Indians, 51, 108
signaling network, 86
Sinagua culture, 20, 27, 36, 40, 41, 43
Sky City, 67
Slaughter Canyon, 77
Smoki Museum, 36
Snake Indians, 51
Snake River, 179, 180, 182, 185
Snaketown Site, 15, 23, 41
South Fork Pictographs, 121
Southwest, defined, 22
Spanish explorers, 33, 67, 86, 92, 95, 99, 103, 105
Spanish Missions, 67, 92, 93, 99
Spider Rock, 8
Spruce Tree House, 57–58
Square Tower Group, 118, 119
Squash Blossom Girl, 98
stratigraphy, 116
Sun Dagger, 85
Sun Point Pueblo, 58

Sun Temple, 58
Sunset Crater, 41, 42
Sunset Crater National Monument, 36, 43

Taos Indians, 48
Taos Pueblo, 103
technology, 15, 46, 49, 58, 61, 63, 122
teepee, mud, 117
Thompson Wash Petroglyphs, 122
Three Kiva Pueblo, 122
Three Rivers Petroglyphs, 104
Three Turkey Ruin Tribal Park, 37
Tiwa language, 86, 99
Tohono o'odham Indians, 6, 35
Tompiro Language, 67
Tonto National Monument, 16, 37–39
tools: adze, 6; ax, 6; atlatls and darts, 102; bow and arrows, 102; celt, 6; crutches, 59; darts, 102; flesher, 62; hafting, 6–7; mesquite gum, 18; points, fluted, 89, Sandia, 101; sharpening, 79; shields, 114; throwing stick, 102; See also agriculture; cooking practices; weaving; women's activities
Topoc Maze, 39
Towa language, 93
towers, 56, 61, 101, 108, 111, 118, 119, 120
trade: Southwest, 5, 25, 27, 52, 67, 81, 96
trails: exhibit, 34, 71, 86, 118; Indian, 73; roads, 81, 82, 83
transportation: travois, 25
"Tree-ring Dating," 106
Tsankawi, 71
tuff, 72
Turner, Christy G., II, 15
turquoise, 18, 15, 52
Tusayan Ruin, 21, 23
Tuzigoot National Monument, 40, 41
Twin Angels Pueblo, 104
Twin War Gods, 48

Tyuonyi, 71, 72

United Nations, 36
University of Arizona, 20, 26, 40–41
University of New Mexico, Maxwell Museum, 101, 104
University of Utah, 122
Utah Field House of Natural History, 122
Utah Museum of Natural History, 123
Ute Indian Museum, 64
Ute Indians, 51, 61, 114, 123
Ute Mountain Tribal Park, 64
Ute Mountain Ute Indians, 64; Park, 50

vandalism, 44
Ventana Cave, 41
Verde River, 27, 40
Vickery, Irene, 16
village development, 3–11 passim, 55–61
Village of the Great Kivas, 105
Village Vista Site, 104
visiting excavations, 25, 26, 33, 50, 115, 123. See also field schools; volunteering
Vivian, R. Gwinn, 84
volcanic eruptions, 36, 41, 42, 43, 96
volunteering, 20. see also field schools

Walnut Canyon National Monument, 11, 41
Walnut Canyon, New Mexico, 77
Walpi, 42
weaponry: Sandia points, 101; other, 102. See also Clovis Points; Folsom points
"Weather Prediction," 122
weaving, 21, 37, 56, 63; looms, 57
Western Archaic; Southwestern, 4, 7, 22
Western New Mexico University Museum, 104

Westwater Creek, 112
Westwater Five Kiva Ruin, 123
Wetherill, Clayton, 116
Wetherill, John, 30, 116
Wetherill Mesa, 45, 55, 58, 61, 62, 63
Wetherill, Richard, 30, 54, 59, 61, 116
wheelchair access, 47, 115. See also handicapped access
White House Ruins, 8, 16
White Mesa Institute, 123
White Mountain Apache Indians, 25
women's activities, 48, 55, 56
Works Progress Administration, 16
World Heritage Sites, 21, 36, 55, 78
Wupatki National Monument, 36, 41, 42–43

Yellow Jacket area, 46, 50
Yucca House National Monument, 61
Yuma Indians, 7

Zia Pueblo, 104
Zion National Park, 123
Zuni Indians, 33, 40, 87, 105
Zuni Pueblo, 105